Laugh Your Lips Off!

A delightfully fresh compilation of
silly stories, amusing anecdotes, rib-tickling
jokes and more, sure to leave you smiling!

by Jenny Herrick
with Kathy Hoeschen Massey

The jokes and material contained in this book have been collected by Jenny Herrick from various sources (friends, enemies, audience members, fellow speakers, nurses, a few doctors, strangers in strange places!) over a number of years. It is Jenny's goal to include only material she finds "clean and clever and something I'd be proud to share with my audiences." Sincere effort was made to attribute material within this book to original authors. If we failed to do so, we hope you will forgive us and appreciate our effort to share this content with our audience.

For additional copies of this book, or for other products offered by Jenny Herrick, please visit Jenny Herrick's website: www.allkiddingaside.biz
or e-mail her at: jenny@allkiddingaside.biz

Laugh Your Lips Off! by Jenny Herrick
with Kathy Hoeschen Massey.

ISBN: 978-0-9794317-1-5

Published by All Kidding Aside, Sioux City, IA.
Cover and text printed by Pacific City Graphics,
South Sioux City, Nebraska.

Cover Design: Kathy Hoeschen Massey,
Design On The Side, Sioux City, Iowa.

Eric Lee Martin ~ 1960-2011

Dedication

This book is dedicated in memory of my son, Eric Lee Martin.

This is a fitting tribute to a man adored by all whose lives he touched. People who came into contact with Eric thought of him as a role model, a super nice guy, a mentor, a terrific boss, an encourager, a fun-lover and much more.

But especially, my Eric was known as a loyal and compassionate friend.

Eric touched more lives in his short time on earth than many people touch in a lifetime.

As he became an adult, Eric grew to become my friend, sometimes even my confidante, for there were times he seemed wiser and more mature than me. He had a way of helping me look at situations in a new and different light.

I so looked forward to and enjoyed our super-lengthy Sunday night phone visits ... I guess it's true that a mother is all those things you never outgrow your need for.

Eric and I shared a common interest until the day he died — the extreme love of dogs. My heart swelled with pride when he would phone to ask my opinion about something regarding his dogs.

Can you imagine how pleased I was when Eric entrusted ME to find him a Golden Retriever show puppy? To put icing on the cake, he named that beautiful puppy after me! With many hours of hard work and training, "Jenny-dog" turned out to be a "top" obedience contender in the show ring!

Eric was the one person who knew how to brighten my day and make my heart smile. (FYI-he won the Port of Sioux City Rivercade Smile Contest at age 8!)

A smile takes but a moment, but its memory lasts forever.

Losing a child is beyond the reach of a parent's imagination, and my boy will live in my memories and my heart forever.

Rest in peace, my baby boy ... Love you, Mom

(Eric passed away from colon cancer. For those of you who are not aware, five days after we celebrated Eric's first birthday, his father died in a work accident.)

Acknowledgements

To everyone who has ever pulled me aside and whispered, "Jenny, I've got a good one for ya!" and anyone who has ever pushed "forward" on an e-mail that made them smile, I say thanks!

To all my audiences who have ever snorted coffee through their nostrils, buckled over in laughter or otherwise encouraged me to keep sharing my message that humor is indeed the best medicine, I say thanks.

To my family, who put up with me through this writing process and continue to make me smile, every day, I say thanks!

To the fine people at Pacific City Graphics, who turn my words into this adorable little book and who work with me through all my last-minute tweaking without ever squeaking, I say thanks!

Finally, I can't express adequate words to thank Kathy Hoeschen Massey for the talent and effort she brought to this book. Without her tenacious devotion, you would not be reading this delightful little book! So what you read here is my book AND hers!

Thank you, dear Kathy ... you are a gem!

6 / Laugh Your Lips Off!

Table of Contents

Chapter   **Page**

1. Furry and Feathered Funnies 9
2. From the (Grinning) Mouths of Babes 17
3. Why Are We Here? 27
4. I've Been a Good Mom All Year 31
5. 25 Things My Mother Taught Me 39
6. Apparently Parenting is Funny 43
7. Letter from Boot Camp 47
8. A List to Live By 51
9. Classroom Cut-ups 53
10. One Plus One Makes ... Fun! 61
11. One for the Fellas 71
12. Beyond Murphy's Law 75
13. Sincerely, the Management 79
14. Prescription for Laughs 93
15. Remember When? 99
16. Having a Senior Moment? 105
17. A Little Holy Humor 113
18. Assorted Grins, Giggles & Guffaws 123
19. A Few for the Ole & Lena Fans 133
20. Sending You Off With a Smile 139

8 / Laugh Your Lips Off!

> *"If you think dogs can't count, try putting three dog biscuits in your pocket and then giving Fido only two of them."* — Phil Pastoret

1

Furry & Feathered Funnies

- If you can start the day without caffeine,
- If you can always be cheerful, ignoring aches and pains,
- If you can resist complaining and boring people with your troubles,
- If you can eat the same food every day and be grateful for it,
- If you can understand when your loved ones are too busy to give you any time,

10 / Laugh Your Lips Off!

- If you can take criticism and blame without resentment,
- If you can conquer tension without medical help,
- If you can relax without liquor,
- If you can sleep without the aid of drugs,
- Then you are probably... the family dog!

✧ ✧ ✧ ✧ ✧

A lady was walking down the street to work and she saw a parrot in a pet store. The parrot said to her, "Hey lady, you are really ugly." Well, the lady was furious! And she stormed past the store to her work.

On the way home she saw the same parrot in the window and the parrot said to her, "Hey lady, you are really ugly." Well, she was incredibly ticked now. The next day she saw the same parrot and the parrot said to her, "Hey lady, you are really ugly."

The lady was so ticked that she went into the store and said that she would sue the store and kill the bird. The store manager said, "That's not good" and promised the bird wouldn't say it again. When the lady walked past the store after work, the parrot said to her, "Hey lady." She paused and said, "Yes?" and the bird said, "You know."

✧ ✧ ✧ ✧ ✧

Returning home from work, a blonde was shocked to find her house ransacked and burglarized. She called the police at once and reported the crime. The police dispatcher broadcast the call on the channels, and a K-9 unit patrolling nearby was the first to respond.

As the K-9 officer approached the house with his dog on a leash, the blonde ran out on the porch, shuddered at the sight of the cop and his dog, and then sat down on the steps.

Putting her head in her hands, she cried, "I come home to find all my possessions stolen. I call the police for help, and what do they do? Send me a BLIND policeman!"

✧ ✧ ✧ ✧ ✧

An older, tired-looking dog wandered into my yard; I could tell from his collar and well-fed belly that he had a home and was well taken care of.

He calmly came over to me. I gave him a few pats on his head; he then followed me into my house, slowly walked down the hall, curled up in the corner and fell asleep.

An hour later, he went to the door, and I let him out.

The next day he was back, greeted me in my yard, walked inside and resumed his spot in the hall and again slept for about an hour. This continued off and on for several weeks.

Curious, I pinned this note to his collar: "I would like to find out who the owner of this wonderful sweet dog is and ask if you are aware that almost every afternoon your dog comes to my house for a nap."

12 / Laugh Your Lips Off!

The next day he arrived for his nap, with a different note pinned to his collar: "His name is Norman and he lives in a home with 6 children, 2 under the age of 3. He's trying to catch up on his sleep. Can I come with him tomorrow?"

✧ ✧ ✧ ✧ ✧

The man had adopted a new dog from the shelter, and was happy with every aspect of the animal's behavior — except for one.

Every time a bell rang — a doorbell, a bell on TV, even when two pieces of silverware clinked together — the dog would go sit in the corner.

So the man explained the situation to his veterinarian, who reassured him the behavior was perfectly normal.

"After all," the vet said, "he is a boxer."

✧ ✧ ✧ ✧ ✧

A man absolutely hated his wife's cat, Sparky. One day he decided to get rid of Sparky by driving him two miles from his home and leaving him at the park. But just as the man arrived back home, the cat was walking up the driveway.

The next day he decided to drive the cat four miles away. He put the beast out of the car and headed home. There, on the front steps, was the cat, waiting for him!

He kept leaving the cat further and further away, and

the cat would always beat him home.

At last he decided to drive a few miles away, turn right, then left, past the bridge, then right again and another right until he reached what he thought was a safe distance from his home and left the cat there.

Hours later the man called home to his wife: "Honey, is Sparky there?"

"Yes", the wife answered. "Why do you ask?"

Frustrated, the man said, "Put that little hairball on the phone. I'm lost and need directions."

✧ ✧ ✧ ✧ ✧

A guy is driving around the back woods of Montana when he sees a sign in front of a broken down shanty-style house:

> TALKING DOG FOR SALE

Curious, he rings the bell and the owner appears and tells him the dog is in the backyard.

The guy goes into the backyard and sees a nice-looking Labrador retriever sitting there.

"You talk?" he asks.

"Sure do," the Lab replies.

14 / Laugh Your Lips Off!

After the guy recovers from the shock of hearing a dog talk, he says, "So, what's your story?"

The dog looks up and says, "Well, I discovered that I could talk when I was pretty young. I wanted to help the government, so I told the CIA. In no time at all they had me jetting from country to country, sitting in rooms with spies and world leaders, because no one figured a dog would be eavesdropping.

"I was one of their most valuable spies for eight years running.

"But the jetting around really tired me out, and I knew I wasn't getting any younger so I decided to settle down. I signed up for a job at the airport to do some undercover security, wandering near suspicious characters and listening in. I uncovered some incredible dealings and was awarded a batch of medals.

"I got married, had a mess of puppies, and now I'm just retired."

The guy is amazed. He asks the owner what he wants for the dog.

"Ten dollars," the guy says.

"Ten dollars? This dog is amazing! Why on earth are you selling him so cheap?"

"Because he's a liar," the owner says. "He's never been out of the yard."

✧ ✧ ✧ ✧ ✧

Life Lessons from a Dog

- Never pass up the chance for a joyride. Enjoy the wind in your face.
- When loved ones come home, run to greet them.
- When it's in your best interest, practice obedience.
- Let others know when they've invaded your territory.
- Take naps and stretch before rising.
- Run, romp and play daily.
- Be loyal.
- Don't pretend to be something you're not.
- If what you want lies buried, dig, dig, dig until you find it. Don't give up!
- When someone is having a bad day, be silent, sit close by and nuzzle them gently.
- Thrive on attention and let people touch you.
- Avoid biting when a simple growl will do.
- On hot days, drink lots of water and take a nap under a shady tree.
- When you're happy, dance around and wag your entire body.
- When you get into trouble, don't waste time pouting. Ask for forgiveness and get over it.
- Delight in the simple joy of a long walk.
- Assume strangers are all just friends you haven't yet met!

16 / Laugh Your Lips Off!

"When my kids become wild and unruly, I use a nice safe playpen. When they're finished, I climb out."
— Erma Bombeck

2
From the (Grinning) Mouths of Babes

From the day they are born, children have the ability to make us smile, giggle, and all-out-snort-our-milk laugh. And they can make us do so just by watching the expressions on their faces while they sleep! Here are some of my favorite silly stories from the younger set:

✧ ✧ ✧ ✧

Little Emma asked Granny how old she was. Granny said she was so old she didn't remember anymore. Emma said, "Just look in the back of your panties, Gran. Mine say '5 to 6.'"

18 / Laugh Your Lips Off!

✧ ✧ ✧ ✧ ✧

A very pregnant woman was home alone with her young daughter when the power went out and her water broke. She called 911. When the paramedics arrived, the little girl, Audrey, answered the door. The paramedics rushed to the mother's side and, as young Audrey held the flashlight, delivered her baby brother.

One paramedic lifted the baby by his feet and spanked his bottom. The baby started to cry. As the other paramedic bundled up the baby, the first turned to Audrey and asked what she thought of what she had seen.

Audrey quickly responded: "He shouldn't have crawled up there in the first place. Spank him again."

✧ ✧ ✧ ✧ ✧

Young Nancy was in the garden filling in a hole with dirt when her crotchety old neighbor peered over the fence. Even though the neighbor didn't much like the kid, he was curious about what she was doing. So he asked, "What are you up to there, Nancy?"

"My goldfish died," Nancy replied tearfully without looking up," and I've just buried him."

The neighbor laughed and said condescendingly, "That's a really big hole for a goldfish, isn't it?"

Nancy tapped the last bit of dirt onto the mound and said, "that's 'cause my goldfish is inside your stupid cat."

✧ ✧ ✧ ✧ ✧

One day a little girl was sitting and watching her mother do the dishes at the kitchen sink. She suddenly noticed that her mother had several strands of white hair sticking out in contrast on her brunette head.

"Why are some of your hairs white, Mom?" she asked.

Her mother replied, "Well, every time that you do something wrong and make me cry or feel unhappy, one of my hairs turns white."

The girl thought about this for a while and then asked, "Mom, how come ALL of grandma's hairs are white?"

✧ ✧ ✧ ✧ ✧

A Sunday school teacher was discussing the Ten Commandments with her 5- and 6-year-olds. After explaining the commandment to "honor" thy Father and thy Mother, she asked, "Is there a commandment that teaches us how to treat our brothers and sisters?"

From the back, one little boy (the oldest of a family) answered, "Thou shall not kill."

✧ ✧ ✧ ✧ ✧

A 7-year-old went to his grandfather, who was working in the yard, and asked him, "Grandpa, what is sex?"

The grandfather was surprised the boy would ask such a question, but decided that if the boy was old enough to ask, he was old enough to get a straight answer. So he proceeded to explain to the boy about human reproduction.

20 / Laugh Your Lips Off!

When he finished explaining, the boy just stared at his grandfather, eyes wide in amazement.

Seeing this look, the grandfather asked, "Boy, why did you want to know what sex was?"

"Because Grandma says dinner will be ready in just a couple of secs," the still-wide-eyed boy replied.

✧ ✧ ✧ ✧ ✧

A teacher was giving a lesson on blood circulation. Trying to make the matter clearer, she said, "Now, class, if I stood on my head, the blood, as you know, would run into it, and I would turn red in the face."

"Yes," the class said.

"Then why is it that while I am standing upright in a normal position, the blood doesn't run into my feet?"

A little fellow shouted, "Cause your feet ain't empty."

✧ ✧ ✧ ✧ ✧

The children were lined up in the cafeteria of a Catholic elementary school for lunch. At the head of the table was a pile of apples. The nuns had posted this note on the apple tray:

> PLEASE TAKE ONLY ONE.
> GOD IS WATCHING!

Moving further along the lunch line, at the other end of the table was a large pile of chocolate chip cookies. A little boy elbowed his friend and said, "Take all you want. God is watching the apples...."

✧ ✧ ✧ ✧ ✧

I returned home from a business trip just when a storm hit with crashing thunder and lightning. As I came into my bedroom, I found my two children in bed with my wife, apparently scared by the loud storm. I resigned myself to sleep in the guest bedroom that night.

The next day, I told the children that it was OK to sleep with Mom when the storm was bad, but when I was expected home, please don't sleep with Mom that night. They said OK.

After my next trip a few weeks later, my wife and children picked me up in the terminal at the appointed time. As I entered the waiting area, my son came running shouting, "Hi, Dad! I've got good news!"

As I waved back, I said loudly, "What's the good news?" "Nobody slept with Mommy while you were away this time!" Alex shouted. The airport became very quiet, as everyone in the waiting area looked at Alex, then turned to me, and then searched the rest of the area to see if they could figure out exactly who his Mom was.

✧ ✧ ✧ ✧ ✧

22 / Laugh Your Lips Off!

A first-grader was sitting at the kitchen table, eating his after-school snack, when he blurted out: "Mom, the teacher was asking me today if I have any brothers or sisters who will be coming to school."

The boy's mother replied, "That's nice of her to take such an interest, dear. What did she say when you told her you were an only child?"

"She just said, 'Thank goodness!'"

✧ ✧ ✧ ✧

(An oldie but a goodie from the days before cell phones):

Mother had been gone all weekend at a business conference. During a break, she decided to call home "collect."

Six-year-old Miles picked up the phone and heard a stranger's voice say, "We have a Marcia on the line. Will you accept the charges?"

Frantic, Miles dropped the phone and went running to his father, "Dad! They've got Mom and they want money!"

✧ ✧ ✧ ✧

The little boy was waiting on his mother to come out of a store. As he waited, he was approached by a man who asked, "Son, can you tell me where the post office is?"

"Sure," the little boy replied. "Just go straight down the street a couple blocks and turn right."

The man thanked the boy and said, "By the way, I'm the new preacher in town and I'd like for you to come to church on Sunday. I'll show you how to get to heaven!"

"Aw, come on," the little boy replied with a laugh. "You don't even know how to get to the post office!"

✧ ✧ ✧ ✧ ✧

A father and son went fishing one day. While in the boat, the boy suddenly became curious about the world around him. So he asked his pop, "Dad, how does this boat float?"

"Well, I don't rightly know, son," the man said.

A bit later, the boy asked, "How do fish breathe underwater?"

"Don't rightly know, son," his father said.

A few minutes passed before the little boy asked, "Dad, why is the sky blue?"

"Again, the father answered, "Don't rightly know, son."

Finally, the little boy asked, "Dad, do you mind me asking you all these questions?"

The father replied, "Of course not, son. If you don't ask any questions, you're never gonna learn nothin'."

✧ ✧ ✧ ✧ ✧

24 / Laugh Your Lips Off!

A young farm boy accidentally overturned his wagon load of wheat on the road. He was sitting dejectedly atop the tossed load when a farmer who lived nearby came to investigate.

Seeing the boy's long face, the farmer called out, "Hey, Teddy, forget your troubles for awhile and come have dinner with us. Then I'll help you right the wagon."

"That's very nice of you," Teddy said, "but I don't reckon Pa would like me to."

"Aw, come on, son, the wagon ain't going nowhere," the farmer insisted.

"OK," the boy finally agreed, "but Pa won't like it."

After dinner, Teddy thanked his hosts, then added, "I feel a lot better right now, but I know Pa's gonna be real upset."

"Don't be silly," said the farmer. "By the way, where is your pa?"

"Under the wagon," replied little Teddy.

✧ ✧ ✧ ✧ ✧

Little Cameron and his family were having Sunday dinner at his Grandmother's house. Everyone was seated at the table as the food was being served. When Cameron received his plate, he began eating right away.

"Cameron, wait 'til we say our prayers!" his mother said.

"I don't have to," the boy replied.

"Of course you do," his mother insisted, embarrassed at her son's apparent disobedience. "We say a prayer at Grandma's before eating, just like we do at our house."

"Aw, that's our house," Cameron explained. "But this is Grandma's house — and we don't have to pray because she knows how to cook!"

✧ ✧ ✧ ✧ ✧

Mother decided 10-year-old Emily should get something "practical" for her birthday. "Suppose we open a savings account for you?" she suggested. Emily was delighted.

"It's your account, dear," mother said as they arrived at the bank, "so you fill out the application."

Little Emily was doing just fine until she came to the space for "Name of your former bank." After a slight hesitation, she wrote down, "Piggy."

✧ ✧ ✧ ✧ ✧

A little girl became restless as the preacher's sermon dragged on and on. Finally, she leaned over to her mother and whispered — much too loudly for her mother's comfort — "Mommy, if we give him the money, will he let us go?"

✧ ✧ ✧ ✧ ✧

26 / Laugh Your Lips Off!

I was taking my 8-year-old daughter to sell cookies door-to-door for the Girl Scouts. After visiting several homes, she commented on the different doorbell styles: some buzzed, some rang, some warbled. We made a game of guessing what the next bell would be like.

At the moment she touched the doorbell at one house, the church tower across the street began to chime.

My daughter wheeled around with an amazed look, saying, "Now *that's* a doorbell!"

✧ ✧ ✧ ✧ ✧

A Sunday School teacher asked a little boy, "Bobby, do you believe in the devil?"

"Nah," Bobby said. "He's just like Santa Claus and the Easter Bunny. I think it's my daddy."

✧ ✧ ✧ ✧ ✧

A heavy snowstorm lasting several days closed the schools for nearly a week. When the children returned to class a few days later, one third-grade teacher at a Lutheran school asked her students whether they had used the time from school constructively.

"I sure did, teacher," one little girl replied. "I prayed."

"Well that's wonderful, dear," her teacher said. "Do you mind if I ask what you prayed for?"

"Sure," said the little girl. "I prayed for more snow."

✧ ✧ ✧ ✧ ✧

> *"To be in your children's memories tomorrow, you have to be in their lives today."*
> — Anonymous

3
Why Are We Here?

So we were lying on our backs on the grass in the park next to our hamburger wrappers, my 14-year-old son and I, watching the clouds loiter overhead, when he asked me, "Dad, why are we here?"

And this is what I said:

"I've thought a lot about it, son, and I don't think it's all that complicated. I think maybe we're here just to teach a kid how to bunt or eat sunflower seeds without using his hands.

"We're here to pound the steering wheel and scream as we listen to the game on the radio, 20 minutes after

28 / Laugh Your Lips Off!

we pulled into the garage. We're here to look all over, give up, and then find the ball in the hole.

"We're here to wear our favorite sweat-soaked Boston Red Sox cap, torn Slippery Rock sweatshirt, and the Converse sneakers we lettered in on a Saturday morning with nowhere we have to go and no one special we have to be.

"We're here to tie the perfect fly, make the perfect cast, catch absolutely nothing, and still call it a perfect morning. We're here to nail a yield sign with an apple core from half a block away. We're here to win the stuffed bear or go broke trying.

"I don't think the meaning of life is gnashing our bicuspids over what comes after death but tasting all the tiny moments that come before it. We're here to be there when our kid has three goals and an assist. And especially when he doesn't.

"I don't think we're here to make SportsCenter. The really good stuff never does. Like finding ourselves with a free afternoon, a little red 327 fuel-injected 1962 Corvette convertible, and an unopened map of Vermont's back roads.

"None of us will find ourselves on our deathbeds saying, 'I wish I'd spent more time on the Hibbings account.' We're going to say, 'That scar? I got that scar stealing a home run from Consolidated Plumbers!'

"See, grown-ups spend so much time doggedly slaving toward the better car, the perfect house, the big day that will finally make them happy, when happy just walked by wearing a bicycle helmet two sizes too big for him. We're not here to find a way to heaven. The way is heaven.

"Does that answer your question, son?"

And he said, "Not really, Dad."

And I said, "No?"

And he said, "No, what I meant is, why are we here when Mom said to pick her up 40 minutes ago?"

✧ ✧ ✧ ✧ ✧

30 / Laugh Your Lips Off!

> "I want my children to have all the things I couldn't afford. Then I want to move in with them." — *Phyllis Diller*

4
I've Been a Good Mom All Year

Dear Santa,

I've been a good mom all year. I've fed, cleaned and cuddled my children on demand, visited the doctor's office more than my doctor and sold 62 cases of candy bars to raise money to plant a shade tree on the school playground. I was hoping you could spread my list out over several Christmases, since I had to write this letter with my son's red crayon, on the back of a receipt in the laundry room between cycles, and who knows when I'll find any more free time in the next 18 years.

32 / Laugh Your Lips Off!

Here are my Christmas wishes:

I'd like a pair of legs that don't ache (in any color, except purple, which I already have) and arms that don't hurt or flap in the breeze, but are strong enough to pull my screaming child out of the candy aisle in the store.

I'd also like a waist, since I lost mine somewhere.

If you're hauling big ticket items this year, I'd like fingerprint resistant windows and a radio that only plays adult music, a television that doesn't broadcast any programs containing talking animals, and a refrigerator with a secret compartment behind the crisper where I can hide to talk on the phone.

On the practical side, I could use a talking doll that says, "Yes, Mommy" to boost my parental confidence, along with two kids who don't fight and three pairs of jeans that will zip all the way up without the use of power tools.

I could also use a recording of Tibetan monks chanting "Don't eat in the living room" and "Take your hands off your brother," because my voice seems to be just out of my children's hearing range and can only be heard by the dog.

If it's too late to find any of these products, I'd settle for enough time to brush my teeth and comb my hair in the same morning, or the luxury of eating food warmer than room temperature without it being served in a Styrofoam container.

If you don't mind, I could also use a few Christmas miracles to brighten the holiday season. Would it be too much trouble to declare ketchup a vegetable? It will clear my conscience immensely. It would be helpful if you could coerce my children to help around the house without demanding payment as if they were the bosses of an organized crime family.

Well, Santa, the buzzer on the dryer is calling and my son saw my feet under the laundry room door. I think he wants his crayon back. Have a safe trip and remember to leave your wet boots by the door and come in and dry off so you don't catch cold.

Help yourself to cookies on the table but don't eat too many or leave crumbs on the carpet.

Yours always,

MOM...

P.S. One more thing ... you can cancel all my requests if you can keep my children young enough to believe in Santa.

✧ ✧ ✧ ✧ ✧

No matter who you are, chances are you can remember words of motherly wisdom ingrained into your little head as you were growing up. Here are some momisms that could just possibly have been uttered by some famous and infamous persons' moms:

PAUL REVERE'S MOTHER: "I don't care *where* you think you have to go, young man — midnight is past your curfew! Put down those lamps and go to bed!"

34 / Laugh Your Lips Off!

MONA LISA'S MOTHER: "After all that money your father and I spent on braces, that's the biggest smile you can give us?'"

HUMPTY DUMPTY'S MOTHER: "Humpty, If I've told you once, I've told you a hundred times not to sit on the wall. But would you listen to me? Noooo!"

COLUMBUS'S MOTHER: "I don't care what you've discovered Christopher, you could have written!"

BABE RUTH'S MOTHER: "Babe, how many times have I told you — quit playing baseball in the house! That's the third window you've broken this week!"

MICHELANGELO'S MOTHER: "Mike, can't you paint on walls like other children? Do you have any idea how hard it is to get that stuff off the ceiling?"

NAPOLEON'S MOTHER: "All right, Napoleon. If you're not hiding your report card inside your jacket, then take your hand out of there and prove it!"

ABRAHAM LINCOLN'S MOTHER: "Again with the stovepipe hat? Can't you just wear a baseball cap like the other kids?"

BATMAN'S MOTHER: "It's a nice car, Bruce, but do you realize how much the insurance will be?"

GOLDILOCKS' MOTHER: "I've got a bill here for a busted chair from the bear family. You know anything about this, young lady?"

ALBERT EINSTEIN'S MOTHER: "But, Albert, it's your senior picture. Can't you do something about your hair?"

GEORGE WASHINGTON'S MOTHER: "The next time I catch you throwing money across the Potomac, you can kiss your allowance good-bye!"

JONAH'S MOTHER: "That's a nice story, but now tell me where you've really been for the past three days!"

SUPERMAN'S MOTHER: "Clark, your father and I have discussed it, and we've decided you can have your own telephone line. Now will you quit spending so much time in all those phone booths?"

And finally...

THOMAS EDISON'S MOTHER: "Of course I'm proud that you invented the electric light bulb, dear. Now turn off that light and get to bed!"

✧ ✧ ✧ ✧ ✧

Found taped to the bathroom door in a home with several children and one very patient mother:

Dear Kids,

Don't be alarmed, the world isn't coming to an end. I am simply taking a bath. It will take about thirty minutes and will involve soap and water.

Yes, I know how to swim. Even if I didn't, forcing myself to drown in a half-inch of lukewarm water is more work than I've got energy for. (Which reminds me, I'm all for science projects, but the next time you want to see if Play-Doh floats, use cold water.)

36 / Laugh Your Lips Off!

Don't panic if I'm not out right on time. I've heard that people don't dissolve in water and I'd like to test the theory.

While I'm in the tub, I'd like you to remember a few things:

The large slab of wood between us is called a door. Do not bang to hear my voice. I promise that even though you can't see me, I am on the other side. I'm not digging an escape tunnel and running for the border, no matter what I said earlier. I didn't mean it. Honest.

"Later" means at a time when I am no longer naked, wet, and contemplating bubble gum in the blow dryer. I know you have important things to tell me. Please let one of them be that you have invented a new way to blow bubbles, not a new way to add gum to your hair.

Believe it or not, shouting, "TELEPHONE!" through the closed bathroom door will not make the phone stop ringing. Answer it and take a message. Since Amazing Mind-Reading Mom has the day off, you'll need to write that message down. Use paper and a pencil. Do not use your brother and the laundry marker. We can't send him to school with telephone number tattoos.

Water makes me wet, not deaf. I can still tell the difference between the sound of "nothing" and the sound of a child playing the piano with a basketball. I can also hear you tattling at the top of your lungs. I'm choosing NOT to answer you. Don't call your dad at work and tell him I am unconscious in the bathroom. He didn't appreciate it last time. He won't appreciate it this time. Trust me.

No matter how much I would like it, water does not make me forgetful. I remember who you are and why you are grounded. No, you can't go to Shelby's house to play. No, you can't go to Shelby's house to use the bathroom. If someone is in our other bathroom, you will just have to think dry thoughts and wait. Unless you have four feet and a tail, do not think of going outside to "water" the lawn. I know the dog does it. The neighbors don't feel the need to call me when the dog does it.

Unless the house catches on fire, stay inside and keep the doors locked. Do not go outside and throw rocks at the bathroom window to get my attention. I know it works in the movies. This is reality, the place where people don't like to sit in a tub while rocks and broken glass rain in on them. Do not set the house on fire.

Call me if there is an emergency.

Emergencies ARE:

1. Dad has fallen off the roof.
2. Your brother and/or sister is bleeding.
3. There's a red fire truck in front of our house.

Emergencies are NOT:

1. Dad has fallen asleep.
2. Someone on TV is bleeding.
3. There's a red pickup truck in front of our house.

One other thing: Being forced to use the last roll of toilet paper for a towel does not make me happy. It makes me sticky with little white polka dots. In the

38 / Laugh Your Lips Off!

future, when the tub overflows, use a mop to clean up the water instead of every towel in the house. For my sanity's sake, let's pretend it was the tub, OK? No, I don't want to hear the real story. Ever. Especially not while I'm standing in the pool of water you missed.

By the way, all Play-Doh experiments are hereby canceled.

Be good. Entertain yourselves. Yes, you can do both at the same time. Try coloring, playing a game, or paying that stack of bills on the coffee table.

I'll be out soon. Maybe.

Love,

Your Mom

✧ ✧ ✧ ✧ ✧

"Children: You spend the first two years of their life teaching them to walk and talk. Then you spend the next 16 years telling them to sit down and shut up." — Anonymous

25 Things Mother Taught Me

Mother's try to teach us so much in such a relatively short amount of time — after all, most children stop listening the minute they become teen-agers! Regardless of whether you're a mom, a dad, or a child, I know you'll enjoy this little list of some of the real-life lessons learned from Mom:

✧ ✧ ✧ ✧ ✧

1. My mother taught me TO APPRECIATE A JOB WELL DONE: *"If you're going to kill each other, do it outside. I just finished cleaning."*

40 / Laugh Your Lips Off!

2. My mother taught me RELIGION. *"You better pray that will come out of the carpet."*

3. My mother taught me about TIME TRAVEL. *"If you don't straighten up, I'm going to knock you into the middle of next week!"*

4. My mother taught me LOGIC. *"Because I said so, that's why."*

5. My mother taught me MORE LOGIC. *"If you fall out of that swing and break your neck, you're not going to the store with me."*

6. My mother taught me FORESIGHT. *"Make sure you wear clean underwear in case you're in an accident."*

7. My mother taught me IRONY. *"Keep crying, and I'll give you something to cry about."*

8. My mother taught me about the science of OSMOSIS. *"Shut your mouth and eat your supper."*

9. My mother taught me about CONTORTIONISM. *"Will you look at that dirt on the back of your neck!"*

10. My mother taught me about STAMINA. *"You'll sit there until all that spinach is gone."*

11. My mother taught me about WEATHER. *"This room of yours looks as if a tornado went through it."*

12. My mother taught me about HYPOCRISY. *"If I said it once, I've said it a million times. Don't exaggerate!"*

13. My mother taught me the CIRCLE OF LIFE. *"I brought you into this world, and I can take you out."*

14. My mother taught me about BEHAVIOR MODIFICATION. *"Stop acting like your father!"*

15. My mother taught me about ENVY. *"There are millions of less fortunate children in this world who don't have wonderful parents like you do."*

16. My mother taught me about ANTICIPATION. *"Just wait until we get home."*

17. My mother taught me about RECEIVING. *"You are going to get it when you get home!"*

18. My mother taught me MEDICAL SCIENCE. *"If you don't stop crossing your eyes, They are going to freeze that way."*

19. My mother taught me ESP. *"Put your sweater on; don't you think I know when you are cold?"*

20. My mother taught me HUMOR. *"When that lawn mower cuts off your toes, don't come running to me."*

21. My mother taught me HOW TO BECOME AN ADULT. *"If you don't eat your vegetables, you'll never grow up."*

22. My mother taught me GENETICS. *"You're just like your father."*

23. My mother taught me about my ROOTS. *"Shut that door behind you. Were you born in a barn?"*

24. My mother taught me WISDOM. *"When you get to be my age, you'll understand."*

25. My mother taught me about JUSTICE. *"One day you'll have kids, and I hope they turn out just like you!"*

✧ ✧ ✧ ✧ ✧

Vincent Van Gogh's Family Tree

- His dizzy aunt — Verti Gogh
- The brother who loved to eat prunes — Gotta Gogh
- The brother who worked at a convenience store — Stoppin Gogh
- The grandfather from Yugoslavia — Hu Gogh
- His magician uncle — Where-diddy Gogh
- His Cousin from Mexico — Ah Mee Gogh
- The Mexican cousin's American half-brother — Gring Gogh
- The nephew who drove a stage coach — Wells-Far Gogh
- The constipated uncle — Kant Gogh
- The ballroom dancing aunt — Tang Gogh
- The bird lover uncle — Flamin Gogh
- The fruit-loving cousin — Man Gogh
- An aunt who taught positive thinking — Waydoo Gogh
- The little bouncy nephew — Poe Gogh
- A sister who loved disco — Go Gogh
- And his niece who travels the country in an RV — Winnie Bay Gogh

I saw you smiling ... so there ya Gogh!

"Like all parents, my husband and I just do the best we can, and hold our breath, and hope we've set aside enough money to pay for our kids' therapy." — Michelle Pfeiffer

6
Apparently Parenting is Funny

What did the mother firefly say to her husband while looking at their son?

"Bright for his age, isn't he?"

✧ ✧ ✧ ✧ ✧

Young Cody finished summer vacation and went back to school. Two days later, his teacher phoned his mother to tell her that Cody was misbehaving.

"Wait a minute!" said Cody's mom. "I had him here for nearly three months and I never once called YOU when he misbehaved!"

44 / Laugh Your Lips Off!

✧ ✧ ✧ ✧ ✧

Mom to teen daughter: "Just because we live in a ranch house is no excuse for your room to look like a stable."

✧ ✧ ✧ ✧ ✧

Martin had just received his brand new drivers' license. The entire family headed out to the driveway and climbed into the car so he could take them for a ride for the first time.

Dad immediately headed to the back seat, directly behind the newly minted driver.

"I'll bet you're back there to get a change of scenery after all those months sitting in the front passenger seat teaching me how to drive," says the beaming boy to his father.

"Nope," replies Dad. "I'm gonna sit here and kick the back of your seat as you drive, just like you've been doing to me all these years."

✧ ✧ ✧ ✧ ✧

A father and his 5-year-old son were becoming quite the regulars at the local baseball stadium.

Dad didn't realize how much time they'd been spending at the ball park until one Sunday in church, around Independence Day, when "The Star-Spangled Banner" was on the list of songs. As the organ's notes faded following the congregation's rendition of that same song, the little boy hollared, "Play ball!"

✧ ✧ ✧ ✧ ✧

A boy was watching his father, a pastor, write a sermon.

"How do you know what to say?" the little boy asked.

"God tells me," his wise father said.

"Oh ..." the little boy thought a bit before asking his dad, "then why do you keep crossing things out?"

✧ ✧ ✧ ✧ ✧

Little Russell's parents — figuring it was never too early to get started steering the child in the direction for a successful career — had been talking to him about what he wanted to be when he grew up.

"Do you want to be a doctor, like your mommy?" his mother asked eagerly.

"No, I don't think so," the little boy said with a thoughtful look on his face. "I don't want to be around sick people all the time."

"Then how about a teacher, like your dad?" asked his father with the same eagerness his wife had shown in hopes his child would follow in his footsteps.

"Nah, I don't think so," said Russell, as he held a finger to his chin contemplatively. "You are always grading papers at night, and I don't think that'd be much fun."

"So what do you want to be when you grow up?" his parents said simultaneously.

46 / Laugh Your Lips Off!

"A pastor," the boy said decisively.

While this was unexpected, both parents were pleased that their son would choose such a noble path.

"That's great!" said his dad. "Why do you want to be a pastor?"

"Well, I figure I only have to work one day a week on Sundays," said the little boy. "Plus, since I have to be in church already, I figure it will be more fun to stand up and yell than just have to sit there and listen."

✧ ✧ ✧ ✧ ✧

Kevin ran into the house and grabbed a glass of lemonade after a day of playing with the new kids next door.

"Dad," he piped up, "what's that thing called when two people are sleeping in the same room and one is on top of the other?"

His dad was a bit taken aback, but, realizing this could be a "teachable moment," said, "that's called 'sexual intercourse,' son."

"Oh, 'sexual intercourse,'" the boy repeated. Then, he was back out the door to play with his new friends.

A few minutes later, Kevin was back. "Oh Daaaad," he said in a frustrated tone. "It is NOT called 'sexual intercourse!' It's called 'bunk beds.' And the new kids' mom wants to talk to you."

✧ ✧ ✧ ✧ ✧

> *"If your parents never had children, chances are you won't, either."* — Dick Cavett

7

Letter From Boot Camp

Being from the Midwest, I know we're tough stock. This eye-opening letter, purported to be *"from an Iowa farm kid at Marine Corps training,"* proves just how tough:

✧ ✧ ✧ ✧

Dear Mom and Pop,

I am well. Hope you are. Tell Brother Walt and Brother Elmer the Marine Corps beats working for old man Graffender by a mile. Tell them to join up quick before all of the places are filled.

48 / Laugh Your Lips Off!

I was restless at first because you got to stay in bed till nearly 6 A.M. but I am getting so I like to sleep late.

Tell Walt and Elmer all you do before breakfast is smooth your cot, and shine some things. No hogs to slop, feed to pitch, mash to mix, wood to split, fire to lay. Practically nothing.

Men got to shave but it is not so bad, there's warm water. Breakfast is strong on trimmings like fruit juice, cereal, eggs, bacon, etc., but kind of weak on chops, potatoes, ham, steak, fried eggplant, pie and other regular food, but tell Walt and Elmer you can always sit by the two city boys that live on coffee. Their food plus yours holds you till noon when you get fed again.

It's no wonder these city boys can't walk much. We go on "route marches," which the platoon sergeant says are long walks to harden us. If he thinks so, it's not my place to tell him different. A "route march" is about as far as to our mailbox at home. Then the city guys get sore feet and we all ride back in trucks.

The country is nice but awful flat. The sergeant is like a school teacher. He nags a lot. The Captain is like the school board. Majors and colonels just ride around and frown. They don't bother you none.

This next will kill Walt and Elmer with laughing. I keep getting medals for shooting. I don't know why. The bulls-eye is near as big as a chipmunk head and don't move, and it ain't shooting at you like the Harklau boys at home. All you got to do is lie there all comfortable and hit it. You don't even load your own cartridges.

They come in boxes.

Then we have what they call hand-to-hand combat training. You get to wrestle with them city boys. I have to be real careful though, they break real easy. It ain't like fighting with that ole bull at home. I'm about the best they got in this except for that Bub Vote from over in Hardy. I only beat him once. He joined up the same time as me, but I'm only 5'6" and 130 pounds and he's 6'8" and near 300 pounds dry.

Be sure to tell Walt and Elmer to hurry and join before other fellers get onto this setup and come stampeding in.

Your loving daughter,

Carol

✧ ✧ ✧ ✧ ✧

50 / Laugh Your Lips Off!

"Laughter is like changing a baby's diaper — it doesn't permanently solve any problems, but it makes things more tolerable for a while." — Anonymous

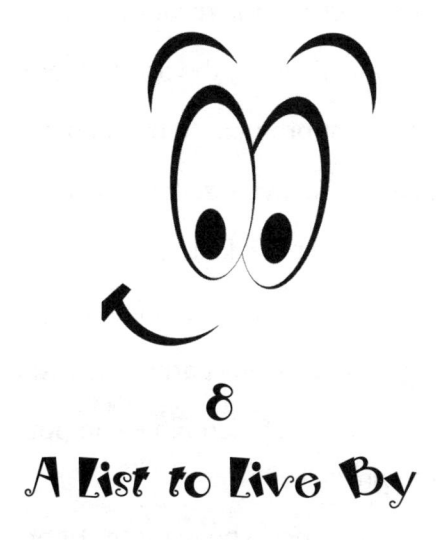

8
A List to Live By

We make lists for shopping. We make lists for our "honeys" to "do." We make lists of what to tell our doctors about our aches and pains.

But how often do we make a list to live by?

Here is a list I am certain you will find yourself referring to time and again as you seek to maximize smiles and minimize negative attitudes in your OWN life and the lives of those around you:

- The most destructive habit: Worry
- The greatest joy: Giving

52 / Laugh Your Lips Off!

- The greatest loss: The loss of self-respect
- The most satisfying work: Helping others
- The ugliest personality trait: Selfishness
- The most endangered species: Dedicated leaders
- Our greatest natural resource: Our youth
- The greatest shot in the arm: Encouragement
- The greatest problem to overcome: Fear
- The most effective sleeping pill: Peace of mind
- The most crippling failure disease: Excuses
- The most powerful force in life: Love
- The most dangerous pariah: A gossiper
- The world's most incredible computer: The brain
- The worst thing to be without: Hope
- The deadliest weapon: The tongue
- The two most power-filled words: I can
- The greatest asset: Faith
- The most worthless emotion: Self-pity
- The most beautiful attire: A smile
- The most prized possession: Integrity
- The most contagious spirit: Enthusiasm

✧ ✧ ✧ ✧

> *"As long as teachers give tests, there will always be prayer in schools."* — Unknown

9

Classroom Cut-ups

A student at our high school, having had his fill with drawing graph after graph in senior math class, told his teacher, "I'll do algebra, I'll do trig, and I'll even do statistics. But graphing is where I draw the line!"

✧ ✧ ✧ ✧ ✧

The children had all been photographed, and the teacher was trying to persuade each to buy a copy of the group picture. "Just think how nice it will be to look at it when you are all grown up and say, 'There's Jada, she's a lawyer,' or 'That's Michael, he's a doctor.'"

A small voice at the back of the room rang out, "And there's the teacher, she's dead."

54 / Laugh Your Lips Off!

✧ ✧ ✧ ✧ ✧

A grade school teacher asked her students to use the word "fascinate" in a sentence.

Molly piped up, "My family went to my granddad's farm, and we all saw his pet sheep. It was fascinating."

The teacher said, "That was good, but I wanted you to use the word 'fascinate,' not 'fascinating.'"

Tia raised her hand. She said, "My family went to see the Black Hills and I was fascinated."

The teacher said, "Well, that was good, Tia, but I wanted you to use the word 'fascinate,' not 'fascinated.'"

Next, little Johnny raised his hand. The teacher hesitated because she had been burned by Johnny before. She finally decided there was no way he could damage the word "fascinate," so she called on him.

Johnny said, "My aunt Gina has a sweater with ten buttons, but her chest is so big, she can only fasten eight."

The teacher sat down and cried.

✧ ✧ ✧ ✧ ✧

A kindergarten teacher was observing her students during art class. She would occasionally walk around to see each child's work. As she got to one little girl who was working diligently, she asked what the drawing was.

The girl replied, "I'm drawing God."

"But no one knows what God looks like," the teacher said.

Without missing a beat, the little girl said, "They will in a minute."

✧ ✧ ✧ ✧ ✧

An eccentric philosophy professor gave a one-sentence final exam after a semester dealing with a broad array of topics: "Using everything we have learned this semester, prove that this chair does not exist."

Fingers flew, erasers erased, notebooks were filled in furious fashion. Some students wrote over 30 pages in one hour attempting to refute the existence of the chair. One member of the class however, was up and finished in less than a minute.

When the grades were posted, the rest of the group wondered how he could have gotten an "A" when he had barely written anything at all.

His answer consisted of two words: "What chair?"

✧ ✧ ✧ ✧ ✧

As the kindergarteners filed into class, little Philip came up to the teacher and told her that he had found a frog. The teacher asked if the frog was alive or dead. Philip, aged 6, declared that it was dead.

The teacher inquired as to how he could be so sure that it was dead.

56 / Laugh Your Lips Off!

Philip replied, "I pissed in its ear."

Flabbergasted, the teacher demanded, "You did what, Philip Brown?"

Philip explained, "You know, I went to his ear and said, 'PSST!' and it didn't move. So it must be dead."

✧ ✧ ✧ ✧ ✧

A little girl was talking to her teacher about whales. The teacher said it was physically impossible for a whale to swallow a human because even though it was a very large mammal, its throat was very small.

The little girl stated Jonah was swallowed by a whale.

The teacher reiterated that a whale could not swallow a human; it was physically impossible.

The girl said, "When I get to heaven I will ask Jonah."

The teacher asked, "What if Jonah went to hell?"

The little girl replied, "Then you ask him."

✧ ✧ ✧ ✧ ✧

First graders were given the beginning of these cliches, and asked to provide their own endings. The results are often better than the original! Take a look:

1. If at first you don't succeed ... go play.
2. Eat, drink, and ... go to the bathroom.
3. All's fair in ... hockey.

Laugh Your Lips Off! / 57

4. He who laughs last ... didn't understand the joke.
5. People in glass houses ... better not take off their clothes.
6. Don't put all your eggs ... in the microwave.
7. Better to be safe than ... punch a 5th grader.
8. Strike while the ... bug is close.
9. It's always darkest before ...Daylight Savings Time.
10. You can lead a horse to water but ... how?
11. Don't bite the hand that ... looks dirty.
12. A miss is as good as a ... Mister.
13. You can't teach an old dog new ... math.
14. If you lie down with dogs, you'll ... stink in the morning.
15. Love all, trust ... me.
16. The pen is mightier than the ... pigs.
17. An idle mind is ... the best way to relax.
18. Happy the bride who ... gets all the presents.
19. A penny saved is ... not much.
20. Two's company, three's ... the Musketeers.
21. Don't put off till tomorrow what ... you put on to go to bed.
22. Laugh and the whole world laughs with you, cry and ... you have to blow your nose.
23. Children should be seen and not ... spanked or grounded.
24. When the blind leadeth the blind ... get out of the way.

✧ ✧ ✧ ✧ ✧

What the Teacher Says ... (and What the Teacher Really Means)

1. Your son has a remarkable ability in gathering needed information from his classmates. (He was caught cheating on a test).

2. Karen is an endless fund of energy and viability. (The hyperactive monster can't stay seated for five minutes).

3. Fantastic imagination! Unmatched in his capacity for blending fact with fiction. (He's definitely one of the biggest liars I have ever met).

4. Margie exhibits a casual, relaxed attitude to school, indicating that high expectations don't intimidate her. (The lazy thing hasn't done one assignment all term).

5. Her athletic ability is marvelous. Superior hand-eye coordination. (The little creep stung me with a rubber band from 15 feet away).

6. Nick thrives on interaction with his peers. (Your son needs to stop socializing and start working).

7. Your daughter's greatest asset is her demonstrative public discussions. (Classroom lawyer! Why is it that every time I explain an assignment she creates a class argument?)

8. John enjoys the thrill of engaging challenges with his peers. (He's a bully).

9. An adventurous nature lover who rarely misses opportunities to explore new territory. (Your daughter was caught skipping school at the fishing pond).

10. I am amazed at her tenacity in retaining her youthful personality. (She's so immature that we've run out of diapers).

11. Unlike some students who hide their emotion, Charles is very expressive and open. (He must have written the Whiner's Guide to Third Grade).

12. I firmly believe that her intellectual and emotional progress would be enhanced through a year's repetition of her learning environment. (Regretfully, we believe that she is not ready for high school and must repeat the 8th grade).

13. Her exuberant verbosity is awesome! (A mouth that never stops yacking).

60 / Laugh Your Lips Off!

"Some people ask the secret of our long marriage. We take time to go to a restaurant two times a week. A little candlelight, dinner, soft music and dancing. She goes Tuesdays, I go Fridays." — Henny Youngman

10
One Plus One Makes ... Fun!

Two guys were discussing popular family trends on sex, marriage, and values. The first one said, "I didn't sleep with my wife before we got married, did you?"

"I'm not sure," the second fellow replied. "What was your wife's maiden name?"

✧ ✧ ✧ ✧ ✧

A state trooper pulls over a speeding car. The trooper says, "I clocked you at 80 miles per hour, sir."

The driver says, "Gee, officer, I had it on cruise control at 60, perhaps your radar gun needs calibrating."

62 / Laugh Your Lips Off!

Not looking up from her knitting, the wife says: "Now don't be silly dear, you know this car doesn't have cruise control."

As the officer writes out the ticket, the driver looks over at his wife and growls, "Can't you please keep your mouth shut for once?" The wife smiles demurely and says, "You should be thankful your radar detector went off when it did."

As the officer makes out the second ticket for the illegal radar, the driver growls at his wife and says through clenched teeth, "Darn it, woman, can't you keep your mouth shut?"

The officer frowns, saying, "And I notice you're not wearing your seat belt, sir. That's an automatic $75 fine."

The driver says, "Yeah, well, you see officer, I had it on, but took it off when you pulled me over so that I could get my license out of my back pocket."

The wife says, "Now, dear, you know very well that you didn't have your seat belt on. You never wear your seat belt when you're driving."

And as the police officer is writing out the third ticket the driver turns to his wife and barks, "WHY DON'T YOU PLEASE SHUT UP?!?"

The officer looks over at the woman and asks, "Does your husband always talk to you this way, Ma'am?"

The woman looks over at the officer and matter-of-factly responds ... "Only when he's been drinking."

✧ ✧ ✧ ✧ ✧

A husband and wife are getting ready for bed. The wife is standing in front of a full-length mirror taking a hard look at herself.

"You know, dear," she says, "I look in the mirror and see an old woman. My face is all wrinkled, my chest and backside are sagging, I've got fat legs, and my arms are all flabby." She turns to her husband and says, "Tell me something positive to make me feel better about myself."

The husband thinks for a moment, then says in a soft, thoughtful voice, "Well, dear ... there's nothing wrong with your eyesight!"

✧ ✧ ✧ ✧ ✧

A woman was in bed with her lover when she heard her husband opening the front door.

"Hurry!" she said, "Stand in the corner." She quickly rubbed baby oil all over him and then she dusted him with talcum powder. "Don't move until I tell you to," she whispered. "Just pretend you're a statue."

"What's this, honey?" the husband asked as he entered the room. "Oh, it's just a statue," she replied nonchalantly. "The Smiths bought one for their bedroom. I liked the idea so much, I got one for us too."

No more was said about the "statue."

Around two in the morning, the husband got out of bed, went into the kitchen, and returned with a sand-

64 / Laugh Your Lips Off!

wich and a glass of milk. "Here," he said to the "statue." "Eat this. I stood like an idiot at the Smiths for three days and nobody offered me so much as a glass of water."

✧ ✧ ✧ ✧ ✧

A husband and wife were sitting in the living room watching a medical drama when the husband said to his wife, "You know, honey, I never want to live in a vegetative state, dependent on some machine and fluids from a bottle. If that ever happens, just pull the plug."

So the wife got up, unplugged the TV and dumped out her husband's beer.

✧ ✧ ✧ ✧ ✧

A middle-aged couple had two stunningly beautiful teenage daughters. They decided to try one last time for the son they had always wanted. After several months of trying, the wife got pregnant. Nine months later, she delivered a healthy baby boy.

The joyful father rushed into the nursery to see his new son. He took one look and was shocked to see the homeliest baby he had ever laid eyes on. He went to his wife and told her there was no way he could be the father of this child.

"Look at the two beautiful daughters I fathered!" he said. Then he gave his wife a stern look and asked, "Have you been fooling around on me?"

The wife just smiled sweetly and said, "Not this time!"

✧ ✧ ✧ ✧ ✧

Amy and Jane were old friends. They had both been married to their husbands for a long time. Amy was complaining because she felt her husband did not find her attractive anymore.

"As I get older, he doesn't even bother to look at me!" Amy cried.

"I'm so sorry for you," replied Jane, "But frankly, I can't relate. My husband says I get more beautiful every day."

"Yes," Amy said, "but your husband's an antique dealer!"

✧ ✧ ✧ ✧ ✧

A woman told a marriage counselor that her husband's complaint that he "leads a dog's life" was probably well-founded.

"After all," she said, "he comes in the house with muddy feet, then he tracks mud across my clean floors, barks at nothing, growls at his food and makes himself comfortable on my best furniture."

✧ ✧ ✧ ✧ ✧

A woman's husband died. He had $30,000 to his name.

After paying all the funeral expenses, she told her closest friend that there was no money left.

"How can that be? You told me he had $30,000 before he died. How could you be broke?"

66 / Laugh Your Lips Off!

The widow replied, "Well, the funeral cost me $10,000. And I had to make the obligatory donation to the church, pay the organist and pastor and all. That was $1,000. I spent another $500 for the wake, the food and drinks. The rest went for the memorial stone."

"The rest? You mean the memorial stone cost you $18,500? How big was it?"

"Oh," the widow replied, "about three carats."

✧ ✧ ✧ ✧ ✧

An 80-year-old woman was arrested for shoplifting. When she went before the judge, the judge asked her, "What did you steal?"

"A can of peaches," she replied.

The judge asked why she had stolen the peaches, and she said she was hungry. The judge then asked her how many peaches were in the can. She replied, "Six."

"Then I will give you six days in jail," the judge replied.

Before the judge could conclude the trial, the woman's husband asked the judge if he could say something.

"What is it?" the judge asked.

The husband said, "She also stole a can of peas."

✧ ✧ ✧ ✧ ✧

During a vacation, a man's wife is lost at sea while scuba diving. The next day, two police officers visit the man in his hotel room.

"We're sorry to disturb you," says the first. "But we have some information about your wife. Actually, we have some bad news, some pretty good news and some great news. Which would you like to hear first?"

Fearing the worst, the man asks for the bad news first.

"We're sorry to inform you," the policeman says, "that we found your wife's body in the bay this morning."

"Oh my!" the man sobs. Composing himself he remembers what the policeman had said, he asks, "So, what's the good news?"

"When we pulled her up," the eager policeman says, "she had two huge crayfish and a dozen crabs on her."

"What?!" the man exclaims, confused. "And what's the great news?"

"We're going to pull her up again tomorrow!"

✧ ✧ ✧ ✧ ✧

A wife was making a breakfast of fried eggs for her husband. Suddenly her husband burst into the kitchen.

"Careful .... CAREFUL!" he yelled. "Put in more butter. Oh dear, oh dear, WHERE will we get more BUTTER?

68 / Laugh Your Lips Off!

They're going to STICK! Careful, CAREFUL! I said be CAREFUL! You never listen to me when you're cooking! "Turn them! Hurry up! Are you CRAZY? Have you LOST your mind? Don't forget to salt them. You know you always forget to salt them. Use the salt. USE THE SALT!"

The wife just stared at him. "What is WRONG with you?" she asked. "You think I don't know how to fry a couple of eggs after all these years?"

The husband calmly replied, "I just wanted to show you what it feels like when I'm driving with you in the car."

✧ ✧ ✧ ✧ ✧

When our lawn mower broke and wouldn't run, my wife kept hinting to me that I should get it fixed. But, somehow I always had something else to take care of first, the truck, the car, playing golf — always something more important to me.

Finally she thought of a clever way to make her point. When I arrived home one day, I found her seated in the tall grass, busily snipping away with a tiny pair of sewing scissors. I watched silently for a short time and then went into the house. I was gone only a minute, and when I came out again I handed her a toothbrush.

I said, "When you finish cutting the grass, you might as well sweep the driveway."

The doctors say I'll walk again, but I'll always have a limp.

✧ ✧ ✧ ✧ ✧

I got off the phone with a friend who lives in northern North Dakota. She said it had been snowing since early morning and that the snow was waist high and still falling. The temperature was dropping way below zero and the north wind was increasing to near-gale force.

Her husband had nothing to do all day but look through the kitchen window and stare.

She said that if the weather gets much worse, she might just have to let him in.

✧ ✧ ✧ ✧ ✧

The other day, my wife and I got into some petty argument. As is our nature, neither would admit the possibility that we might be the one in error.

To her credit, my wife finally said, "Look, I'll tell you what. I'll admit I'm wrong if you admit I was right."

"Fine," I said.

She took a deep breath, looked me in the eye and said, "I'm wrong."

I grinned and replied, "You're right."

✧ ✧ ✧ ✧ ✧

70 / Laugh Your Lips Off!

"Men want the same thing from their underwear that they want from women: a little bit of support, and a little bit of freedom." — Jerry Seinfeld

11
One for the Fellas

Men are just happier than women. What do you expect from such simple creatures? After all, if you're a man...

- Your last name stays put.
- The garage is all yours.
- Wedding plans take care of themselves.
- Chocolate is just another snack.
- You can never be pregnant.
- Wrinkles add character.
- You can wear a white T-shirt to a water park.
- You can wear NO shirt to a water park.

72 / Laugh Your Lips Off!

- Car mechanics tell you the truth.
- The world is your urinal.
- You never have to drive to another gas station restroom because this one is "just too icky."
- You don't have to stop and think of which way to turn a nut on a bolt. (Lefty loosey, righty tighty.)
- Wedding dress: $5,000. Tux rental: $100.
- People never stare at your chest when you're talking to them.
- The occasional well-rendered belch is practically expected.
- New shoes don't cut, blister, or mangle your feet.
- One mood all the time.
- Phone conversations are over in 30 seconds flat.
- You know stuff about tanks.
- A five-day vacation requires only one suitcase.
- You can open all your own jars.
- You get extra credit for the slightest act of thoughtfulness.
- If someone forgets to invite you, he or she can still be your friend.
- Your underwear is $8.95 for a three-pack.
- Three pairs of shoes are more than enough.
- You almost never have strap problems in public.
- You are unable to see wrinkles in your clothes.
- Everything on your face stays its original color.
- The same hairstyle lasts for years, maybe decades.

- You only have to shave your face and neck.
- You can play with toys all your life.
- Your belly usually hides your big hips.
- One wallet and one pair of shoes one color for all seasons.
- You can wear shorts no matter how your legs look.
- You can "do" your nails with a pocket knife.
- You have freedom of choice concerning growing a mustache.
- You can do Christmas shopping for 25 relatives on December 24 in 25 minutes.

No wonder men are happier than women!

✧ ✧ ✧ ✧ ✧

74 / Laugh Your Lips Off!

> *"Life is too important a thing to ever talk seriously about it."* — Oscar Wilde

12
Beyond Murphy's Law...

You've heard of Murphy's Law: *Everything that can go wrong will... at the worst possible time and in the worst possible way.* There are other related laws of which you may or may not have heard — but have most probably experienced:

- **William's Law:** There is no mechanical problem so difficult that it cannot be solved by brute strength and ignorance.

- **Lorenz's Law of Mechanical Repair:** After your hands become coated with grease, your nose will begin to itch.

76 / Laugh Your Lips Off!

- **Zadra's Law of Biomechanics:** The severity of the itch is inversely proportional to the reach.

- **Beach's Law:** Identical parts aren't.

- **Anthony's Law of the Workshop:** Any tool, when dropped, will roll to the least accessible corner.

- **Lowery's Law:** If it jams, force it. If it breaks, it needed replacing anyway.

- **O'Brien's Variation Law:** If you change lines, the one you have left will start to move faster than the one you are in now.

- **Bell's Theorem:** When the body is immersed in water, the telephone rings.

- **Ruby's Principle of Close Encounters:** The probability of meeting someone you know increases when you are with someone you don't want to be seen with.

- **Willoughby's Law:** When you try to prove to someone that a machine won't work, it will.

- **Breda's Rule:** At any event, the people whose seats are furthest from the aisle arrive last.

- **Wen's Law**: As soon as you sit down to a cup of hot coffee, your boss will ask you to do something which will last until the coffee is cold.

- **Tussman's Law:** Nothing is as inevitable as a mistake whose time has come.

- **Peer's Law:** The solution to a problem changes the problem.

- **IBM's Pollyanna Principle:** Machines should work. People should think.

- **The Dilbert Principle:** The most ineffective workers shall be moved systematically to the place where they can do the least damage.

- **Ehrlich's Law:** The first rule of intelligent tinkering is to save all the parts.

- **Ralph's Observation:** It is a mistake to allow any mechanical object to realize that you are in a hurry.

- **Cannon's Comment:** If you tell the boss you were late for work because you had a flat tire, the next morning you will have a flat tire.

- **Law of inevitable consequences:** The newer the carpet, the greater the likelihood that the bread will land jelly side down.

✧ ✧ ✧ ✧ ✧

> *"The golden rule of work is that the boss's jokes are ALWAYS funny."* — Robert Paul

13

Sincerely, the Management

The average person will spend more than a fourth of his or her lifetime at work. That's why it's so important to find something you love to do, and that people will also pay you to do! I hope you are fortunate enough to have a job you love. And I do know that, love your job or not, it's simple to find ways to smile on the job every day. Here's a few of my favorite work-related stories and jokes:

New Office Policy: Effective Jan. 1

<u>DRESS CODE:</u>

1. You are advised to come to work dressed according to your salary.

80 / Laugh Your Lips Off!

2. If we see you are wearing Prada shoes and carrying a Gucci bag, we will assume you are doing well financially and therefore do not need a raise.

3. If you dress poorly, you need to learn to manage your money better, so that you may buy nicer clothes, and therefore you do not need a raise.

4. If you dress just right, you are right where you need to be and therefore you do not need a raise.

SICK DAYS: We will no longer accept a doctor's statement as proof of sickness. If you are able to go to the doctor, you are able to come to work.

PERSONAL DAYS: Each employee will receive 104 personal days a year. They are called weekends.

BEREAVEMENT LEAVE: There is no excuse for missing work. There is nothing you can do for dead friends, relatives or co-workers. Every effort should be made to have non-employees attend the funeral in your place. In rare cases where employee involvement is necessary, the funeral should be scheduled in late afternoon. We will be glad to allow you to work through your lunch hour and subsequently leave one hour early.

BATHROOM BREAKS: Entirely too much time is being spent in the bathroom. There is now a strict 3-minute time limit in the stalls. At the end of three minutes, an alarm will sound, the toilet paper roll will retract, the stall door will open and a picture will be taken. After your second offense, your picture will be posted on the company bulletin board under the "Chronic Offenders" category. Anyone caught smiling in the picture will be sectioned under the company's mental health policy.

LUNCH BREAK:

1. Skinny people get 30 minutes for lunch, as they need to eat more, so that they can look healthy.

2. Normal-sized people get 15 minutes for lunch to get a balanced meal to maintain their average figure.

3. Chubby people get 5 minutes for lunch, as that is all the time needed to drink a Slim-Fast.

Thank you for your loyalty to our company. We are here to provide a positive employment experience. Therefore, all questions, comments, concerns, complaints, frustrations, irritations, aggravations, insinuations, allegations, accusations, contemplations, consternation and input should be directed elsewhere.

~ Sincerely, the Management

✧ ✧ ✧ ✧ ✧

The door-to-door salesman had not made a sale all week, and it was Friday afternoon. He figured the next house was do-or-die. So he pulled out all the stops and knocked on the door of a tiny, ramshackle house.

A little old lady answered. "What do you want?"

"Well, ma'am, have I got an opportunity for you!" said the young salesman, confidently walking into the woman's modest home before she could protest. "If I could take a couple minutes of your time, I would like to demonstrate the very latest in high-powered vacuum cleaners."

"Go away!" said the old lady. "I haven't got any money," and she proceeded to close the door.

"Don't be too hasty!" he said. "Not until you have at least seen my demonstration."

And with that, he emptied a bucket of horse manure onto her carpet.

Confidently, the salesman proclaimed, "If this vacuum cleaner does not remove all traces of this horse manure from your carpet, Madam, I will personally eat the remainder."

"Well, I hope you have a damned good appetite," the old woman said, "because, like I said, I don't have any money ... and they cut off my electricity this morning."

✧ ✧ ✧ ✧ ✧

Jacob is out sailing in his yacht when he gets into difficulties and radios for assistance. The Coast Guard responds and asks for an accurate fix on the yacht's location.

"What is your position? Repeat, what is your position?"

"My position?" Jacob replies. "Oh, it's a very good one. I'm owner and president of a large manufacturing company!"

✧ ✧ ✧ ✧ ✧

Lawyers should never ask a Mississippi grandma a question unless they are prepared for the answer:

In a trial, a Southern small-town prosecuting attorney called his first witness, a rather elderly woman to the stand. He approached her and asked, "Mrs. Jones, do you know me?"

She responded, "Why, yes I know you, Mr. Williams. I've known you since you were a boy, and frankly, you've been a big disappointment to me. You lie, cheat on your wife, manipulate people and talk about them behind their backs. You think you're a big shot when you haven't the brains to realize you'll never amount to anything more than a two-bit paper pusher. Yes, I know you."

The lawyer was stunned. Not knowing what else to do, he pointed across the room and asked, "Mrs. Jones, do you know the defense attorney?"

She again replied, "Why yes, I do. I've known Mr. Bradley since he was a youngster, too. He's lazy, bigoted, and has a drinking problem. He can't build a normal relationship with anyone, and his law practice is one of the worst in the entire state. Not to mention he cheated on his wife with three different women. One of them was your wife. Yes, I know him."

The attorney nearly died.

The judge asked both counselors to approach the bench and, in a hushed voice said, "If either of you idiots ask this witness if she knows me, I'll send you both to the electric chair."

✧ ✧ ✧ ✧ ✧

84 / Laugh Your Lips Off!

The fellow working the circulation department at the local newspaper was used to calls from angry customers who couldn't find their newspapers, and dispatching a driver to quickly get them a paper.

But he had to think twice about how to solve one caller's dilemma. When he answered the phone, a woman shrieked into his ear, "Where is my Sunday paper, young man?"

After mulling it over a moment or two, the newspaper employee responded as calmly and tactfully as possible, "Ma'am, today is Saturday. The Sunday paper will not be delivered until tomorrow, on SUNDAY."

There was quite a long pause on the other end of the phone, followed by a ray of recognition as he heard the caller mutter, "Well, shoot, so that's why no one was at church today."

✧ ✧ ✧ ✧ ✧

Confiding in a co-worker, I told her about a problem in our office and my fear that I would lose my job. She was concerned and said that she would pray for me. I knew she keeps a list of the 10 people she believes need her prayers the most, so I asked if she had room on that list for me.

"Oh yes," she replied. "Three people on it have died."

✧ ✧ ✧ ✧ ✧

A doctor, an engineer, a rabbi and a lawyer were debating who was the world's first professional.

The doctor said, "It must have been a doctor. Who else could have helped with the world's first surgery of taking a rib from Adam to create Eve, the first woman?"

"No," said the rabbi. "It must have been a rabbi, since the Lord needed someone to help preach his message to Adam and the world."

"Wait," said the engineer. "The world was created in six days from nothing. Do you know what a master engineering feat that must have been to create the whole world into an organized civilized place from utter chaos?"

"And WHO created the chaos?" said the lawyer.

✧ ✧ ✧ ✧ ✧

In the small, family-owned electronics store where my friend works, she often gets folks from out of town whose idioms are a little different from her own. One day, after parking his car across the street in an attended lot, a young man came in. He made his purchase and then asked, "Do you give validation?"

Without batting an eye, my friend replied, "You're an excellent person, and I like how that jacket looks on you."

✧ ✧ ✧ ✧ ✧

86 / Laugh Your Lips Off!

A pastor, a doctor and an engineer were waiting one morning for a particularly slow group of golfers. The engineer fumed, "What's with these guys? We must have been waiting for 15 minutes!"

The doctor chimed in, "I don't know, but I've never seen such ineptitude!"

The pastor said, "Hey, here comes the greens keeper. Let's have a word with him. Hi George. Say, what's with that group ahead of us?"

"They're rather slow, aren't they?" The greenskeeper replied, "Oh, yes, that's a group of blind firefighters. They lost their sight saving our clubhouse from a fire last year, so we always let them play for free anytime."

The group was silent for a moment.

The pastor said, "That's so sad. I think I will say a special prayer for them tonight."

The doctor said, "Good idea. And I'm going to contact my ophthalmologist buddy and see if there's anything he can do for them."

The engineer said, "Why can't these guys play at night?"

✧ ✧ ✧ ✧

A man owned a small ranch in Montana. The Montana Wage & Hour Department claimed he was not paying proper wages to his help and sent an agent out to interview him.

"I need a list of your employees and how much you pay them," demanded the agent.

"Well," replied the rancher, "There's my ranch hand who's been with me for 3 years. I pay him $600 a week plus free room and board. The cook has been here for 18 months, and I pay her $500 per week plus free room and board.

"Then there's the half-wit who works about 18 hours every day and does about 90% of all the work around here. He makes about $10 per week, pays his own room and board and I buy him a bottle of bourbon every Saturday night."

"That's who I want to talk to, the half-wit," said the agent.

"That would be me," replied the rancher.

✦ ✦ ✦ ✦ ✦

Two fellows went into a diner that looked as though it had seen better days. As they slid into a booth, the first fellow wiped crumbs from the seat. Then he took a napkin and wiped some mustard from the table.

The waitress, in a grease-streaked uniform, came over and asked if they wanted some menus.

88 / Laugh Your Lips Off!

"No thanks," said the first fellow. "I'll just have a cup of black coffee."

"I'll have black coffee, too," his friend said. "And please make sure the cup is clean."

The waitress shot him a nasty look. She turned away and marched into the kitchen.

Two minutes later, she was back. "Two cups of black coffee," she announced. "Now which one wanted the clean cup?"

✧ ✧ ✧ ✧ ✧

A passenger in a taxi leaned over and gently tapped the driver's shoulder to ask him a question.

The driver screamed, lost control of the cab, nearly hit a bus, drove up over the curb and stopped just inches from a large plate window.

For a few moments, everything was silent in the cab. Then, the shaking driver said "Are you OK? I'm so sorry, but you scared the daylights out of me."

The badly shaken passenger apologized to the driver and said, "I didn't realize that a mere tap on the shoulder would startle you so badly."

The driver replied, "No, no, I'm the one who is sorry, it's entirely my fault. Today is my very first day driving a cab. I've been driving a hearse for 25 years."

✧ ✧ ✧ ✧ ✧

Laugh Your Lips Off! / 89

Steve got a job as a road-line painter. He paints five miles on the first day, two miles on the second day and one on the third day.

"You get worse and worse every day!" yelled his boss.

"That is because the bucket gets further and further away every day," said Steve.

✧ ✧ ✧ ✧ ✧

Here is an actual list of aircraft problems (P) reported by pilots at the end of the day for the mechanics to fix before takeoff the next day followed by the notes on the solutions (S) the mechanics left for the pilots to read the next morning:

(P) Left inside main tire almost needs replacement
(S) Almost replaced left inside main tire

(P) Something loose in cockpit
(S) Something tightened in cockpit

(P) Evidence of leak on right main landing gear
(S) Evidence removed

(P) DME volume unbelievably loud
(S) Volume set to more believable level

(P) Number three engine missing
(S) Engine found on right wing after brief search

✧ ✧ ✧ ✧ ✧

Signs of Work in Progress

Sign in a Podiatrist's office:
"Time wounds all heels."

On a Plumber's truck:
"We repair what your husband fixed."

On another Plumber's truck:
"Don't sleep with a drip. Call your plumber."

At a Tire Store:
"Invite us to your next blowout."

On an Electrician's truck:
"Let us remove your shorts."

In a Non-smoking Area:
"If we see smoke, we will assume you are on fire and take appropriate action."

On a Maternity Room door:
"Push. Push. Push."

At an Optometrist's Office:
"If you don't see what you're looking for, you've come to the right place."

On a Taxidermist's window:
"We really know our stuff."

On a Fence:
"Salesmen welcome! Dog food is expensive!"

At a Car Dealership:
"The best way to get back on your feet — miss a car payment."

Outside a Car Exhaust Store:
"No appointment necessary. We hear you coming."

In a Veterinarian's waiting room:
"Be back in 5 minutes. Sit! Stay!"

In a Restaurant window:
"Don't stand there and be hungry; come on in and get fed up."

In the front yard of a Funeral Home:
"Drive carefully. We'll wait."

On a Septic Tank Truck:
"Caution — This Truck Full of Political Promises"

And don't forget the sign at a RADIATOR SHOP:
"Best place in town to take a leak."

92 / Laugh Your Lips Off!

> "My doctor is wonderful. Once ... when I couldn't afford an operation, he touched up the X-rays." — Joey Bishop

14
Prescription for Laughs

A man rushed into a busy doctor's office shouting, "Doc! I think I'm shrinking! Ya gotta help me right now!"

"Now settle down," the doctor calmly responded. "You'll just have to be a little patient."

✧ ✧ ✧ ✧ ✧

It was a crazy evening in the ER. The doctor on duty was being bombarded with questions, given forms to fill out, and even being asked for his dinner order.

I was assisting with a patient who had required stitches, and was admiring the doctor's ability to juggle ev-

94 / Laugh Your Lips Off!

erything. That was, until I realized he had not given me instructions about what type of bandage to apply.

As the doctor left the room, I called out, "What kind of dressing do you want on this?"

"Ranch," the doctor yelled back.

✧ ✧ ✧ ✧ ✧

Arriving home, a man was met at the door by his sobbing wife who tearfully said, "It was the pharmacist. He insulted me terribly this morning on the phone."

The man immediately drove in to town to confront the pharmacist and demand an apology.

Before he could say no more than a few words, the pharmacist said, "Now, just a minute, you hold on! Please just listen to my side of it....

"This morning the alarm failed to go off, so I got up late, missed breakfast and ran, half dressed, out to the car, only to realize that I had just locked the house with my keys inside. I had to break a window to get them.

"Then, driving a little too fast, I got a speeding ticket, and then three blocks from the store, I had a flat tire.

"When I got to the store, a line of people was waiting for me to open up, and I started waiting on them, and all the time the stupid phone was ringing off the hook."

The pharmacist continued, "Then breaking a roll of nickels against the cash register drawer to make change, I spilled them all over the floor. I got down on my hands and knees to pick up the nickels; the stupid phone was still ringing. When I came up I cracked my head on the open cash drawer, which made me stagger back against a showcase with a bunch of perfume bottles, and all of them fell to the floor and broke.

"Meanwhile, the stupid phone has not stopped ringing and when I finally answer it, it's your wife, wanting to know how to use a digital rectal thermometer...."

"And, honest, all I did was really tell her!"

✧ ✧ ✧ ✧ ✧

In a hospital's Intensive Care Unit, patients always died in the same bed, on Sunday morning, at about 11 a.m., regardless of their medical condition.

This puzzled doctors and staff and some even thought it had something to do with the supernatural. So a worldwide team of experts assembled to investigate the cause of the incidents.

The next Sunday, a few minutes before 11 a.m., all of the doctors and nurses nervously waited outside the ward to see for themselves what the terrible phenomenon was all about. Some were holding crosses, prayer books, and other holy objects to ward off the evil spirits.

Then, just as the clock struck 11 a.m., the part-time weekend custodian entered the ward, reached over to the outlet panel, and unplugged the life support system so he could use the vacuum cleaner....

✧ ✧ ✧ ✧ ✧

96 / Laugh Your Lips Off!

I went to the doctor for my yearly physical. The nurse started with certain basics.

"How much do you weigh?" she asks. "135," I say.

The nurse puts me on the scale. It says 180.

The nurse asks, "Your height?" "5-foot-5," I say.

The nurse checks and sees that I measure 5-foot-2. She then takes my blood pressure, writes down the numbers, and says, "The doctor will see you in a few minutes."

My doctor comes in and gets straight to the point: "Your blood pressure is very high," she tells me.

"Of course it's high!" I scream, "When I came in here I was tall and slender! Now I'm short and fat!"

The doctor put me on Prozac. Geez. What's her problem?

✧ ✧ ✧ ✧ ✧

In my role as a motivational speaker, I emphasize how humor is truly the best medicine! I challenge people to dare to laugh daily! Why? It's good for your body, your mind and your soul in so many ways! Here are two dozen reasons to laugh ... daily:

1. **A Fresh Perspective:** When you choose humor, you choose to see the world from a different perspective.
2. **A Clean Soul:** What soap is to the body, laughter is to the soul.

3. **A Chance to Feel Alive:** I realized that humor isn't for everyone. It's only for people who want to have fun, enjoy life and feel alive.

4. **Great Publicity:** The tail is the dog's PR department; a smile is yours.

5. **Improved Outlook:** No one ever injured his or her eyesight by looking on the bright side.

6. **Improved Health, too:** Laughter — more powerful than any pill, more potent than an IV drip, more healing than any doctor.

7. **The Chance to Forget Your Worries:** Remember, the optimist laughs to forget; the pessimist forgets to laugh.

8. **Great Circulation:** Humor is a wonderful way to prevent *hardening of the attitudes.*

9. **Success in All Areas of Your Life:** We rarely succeed at anything unless we have fun doing it.

10. **A Lifelong Soundtrack:** Humor is music to the soul, and you need not carry a tune ... just sing along!

11. **A Fresh Outlook:** Humor is the ability to see three sides of the coin.

12. **Hindsight:** It's bad to suppress laughter; it goes back down and spreads your hips.

13. **Foresight:** Laugh at yourself first, before anyone else can.

14. **A Chance to Recycle:** Laugh while you can. There is nothing more biodegradable than happiness.

15. **A Natural Learning Curve:** You don't have to teach people to be funny. You only have to give them permission.

16. **A Beautiful Outlook:** If you could choose one characteristic that would get you through life, choose a positive sense of humor.

17. **A Positively Mindful Perspective:** Most folks are about as happy as they make up their minds to be.

18. **A Chance to Stand Out With the Crowd:** Humorists are serious. They are the only people who are.

19. **Insuring a Future For Our Species:** When humor goes, there goes civilization.

20. **Perspective:** People who laugh at death feel superior to those who are dead.

21. **Life Insurance:** If you are going to tell people the truth, you'd better make them laugh. Otherwise they'll kill you.

22. **The Chance to Fertilize Your Circle of Influence:** A good laugh is like manure to a farmer — it doesn't do any good until you spread it around!

23. **Something in Common With the Big Guy:** Does God have a sense of humor? He must ... He made us!

24. **Health Insurance:** If you don't learn to laugh at trouble, you won't have anything to laugh at when you get old.

> "There are three signs of old age: loss of memory ... I forget the other two." — Red Skelton

15
Remember When?

My Mom used to cut chicken, chop eggs and spread mayonnaise on the same cutting board with the same knife and no bleach, but we didn't seem to get food poisoning.

My Mom used to defrost hamburger on the counter AND I used to eat it raw sometimes, too. Our school sandwiches were wrapped in wax paper in a brown paper bag, not in icepack coolers, but I can't remember getting e.coli.

Almost all of us would have rather gone swimming in the lake instead of a pristine pool (talk about boring).

100 / Laugh Your Lips Off!

The term "cell phone" would have conjured up a phone in a jail cell, and a pager was the school PA system.

We all took gym, not PE ... and risked permanent injury with a pair of high-top Keds (only worn in gym) instead of having cross-training athletic shoes with air cushion soles and built-in reflectors. I can't recall any injuries but they must have happened because they tell us how much safer we are now.

Flunking gym was not an option... even for stupid kids! I guess PE must be much harder than gym.

Speaking of school, we all said prayers and sang the national anthem, and staying in detention after school led to all sorts of negative attention.

We must have had horribly damaged psyches. What an archaic health system we had then. Remember school nurses? Ours wore a hat and everything.

I thought that I was supposed to accomplish something before I was allowed to be proud of myself.

I just can't recall how bored we were without computers, Play Station, Nintendo, X-box or 270 digital TV cable stations.

And where was the Benadryl and sterilization kit when I got that bee sting? I could have been killed!

We played "king of the hill" on piles of gravel left on vacant construction sites, and when we got hurt, Mom pulled out the 48-cent bottle of Mercurochrome (kids liked it better because it didn't sting like iodine did) and then we got our butt spanked.

Now it's a trip to the emergency room, followed by a 10-day dose of a $49 bottle of antibiotics, and then Mom calls the attorney to sue the contractor for leaving a horribly vicious pile of gravel where it was such a threat.

We didn't act up at the neighbor's house either because if we did, we got our butt spanked there and then again when we got home.

I recall the kid from next door coming over and doing his tricks on the front stoop, just before he fell off. Little did his Mom know that she could have owned our house. Instead, she picked him up and swatted him for being such a goof. It was a neighborhood run amok.

To top it off, not a single person I knew had ever been told that they were from a dysfunctional family. How could we possibly have known that?

We needed to get into group therapy and anger management classes? We were obviously so duped by so many societal ills that we didn't even notice the entire country wasn't taking Prozac! How'd we ever survive?

✧ ✧ ✧ ✧ ✧

Someone asked the other day, "What was your favorite fast food growing up?"

"We didn't have fast food when I was growing up," I informed him. "All the food was slow."

"C'mon, seriously. Where did you eat?"

102 / Laugh Your Lips Off!

"It was a place called 'at home,'" I explained. "Mom cooked every day and when Dad got home from work, we sat down together at the dining room table, and if I didn't like what she put on my plate, I was allowed to sit there until I did like it."

By now, the kid was laughing so hard I was afraid he was going to suffer internal damage, so I didn't tell him about how I had to have permission to leave the table.

But here are some other things I would have told him about my childhood if I figured his system could have handled it:

- Some parents NEVER owned their own house, wore Levis, set foot on a golf course, traveled out of the country or had a credit card.

- In their later years they had something called a revolving charge card. The card was good only at Sears Roebuck. Or maybe it was Sears & Roebuck. Either way, there's no Roebuck anymore. Maybe he died.

- My parents never drove me to soccer practice. This was mostly because we never had heard of soccer. I had a bicycle that weighed probably 50 pounds, and only had one speed, (slow).

- We didn't have a TV in our house until I was 5. It was, of course, black and white, and the station went off air at midnight, after playing the national anthem and a poem about God; it came back on the air at 6 a.m. and there was usually a locally produced news and farm show on, featuring local people.

- I was 13 before I tasted my first pizza, it was called "pizza pie." When I bit into it, I burned the roof of my mouth and the cheese slid off, swung down, plastered itself against my chin and burned that, too. It's still the best pizza I ever had.

- We didn't have a car until I was 4. It was an old black Dodge.

- I never had a telephone in my room.

- The only phone in the house was in the living room and it was on a party line. Before you could dial, you had to listen and make sure some people you didn't know weren't already using the line.

- Pizzas were not delivered to our home. But milk was.

- All newspapers were delivered by boys and all boys delivered newspapers — my brother delivered a newspaper, six days a week. It cost 7 cents a paper, of which he got to keep 2 cents. He had to get up at 6 every morning. On Saturday, he had to collect the 42 cents from his customers. His favorite customers were the ones who gave him 50 cents and told him to keep the change. His least favorite customers were the ones who seemed to never be home on collection day.

- Movie stars kissed with their mouths shut. At least, they did in the movies. There were no movie ratings because all movies were responsibly produced for everyone to enjoy viewing, without profanity or

104 / Laugh Your Lips Off!

violence or most anything offensive.

If you grew up in a generation before there was fast food, you may want to share some of these memories with your children or grandchildren. Just don't blame me if they bust a gut laughing.

Growing up isn't what it used to be, is it?

✧ ✧ ✧ ✧ ✧

Fifty Years from Now...

Three elderly gentlemen were talking about what their grandchildren would be saying about them 50 years from now.

"I would like my grandchildren to say, 'He was successful in business,'" said the first man.

"Fifty years from now," the second man said, "I would like my grandchildren to say, 'he was a loyal family man and good provider.'"

"Me?" the third man said. "I want them to say, 'Boy, he looks good for his age!'"

"You know you are getting old when the candles cost more than the cake!"
— Bob Hope

16

Having a Senior Moment?

I've sure gotten old! I've had two bypass surgeries, a hip replacement, and new knees. Fought prostate cancer and diabetes. I'm half blind, can't hear anything quieter than a jet engine, take 40 different medications that make me dizzy, winded and subject to blackouts. Have bouts with dementia. Have poor circulation; hardly feel my hands or feet anymore.

I can't even remember if I'm 85 or 92. I've lost all my friends. But thank goodness, I still have my driver's license.

✧ ✧ ✧ ✧ ✧

106 / Laugh Your Lips Off!

A blue-haired older lady was driving down the highway about 75 miles per hour when she noticed a motorcycle policeman following her. Instead of slowing down, she picked up speed.

When she looked back again, there were two motorcycles following her. She shot up to 90 mph.

The next time she looked around, three police cycles were following her, red lights flashing and sirens blaring.

Suddenly, she spotted a gas station just ahead. She screeched to a stop, hopped out and hobbled into the ladies' room. A few minutes later, she innocently walked out.

The three cops were standing there waiting for her. Without batting an eye, she said coyly, "I'll bet none of you boys thought I'd make it to the bathroom on time!"

✧ ✧ ✧ ✧ ✧

Just before the funeral services, the undertaker came up to the very elderly widow and asked, "How old was your husband?"

"Ninety-eight," the elderly woman replied. "Two years older than me."

"So you're 96," the undertaker commented.

The widow looked around at the funeral parlor, then back at the undertaker and said matter-of-factly, "Hardly worth going home, is it?"

✧ ✧ ✧ ✧ ✧

I'm too old to catch onto all the drug lingo nowadays. I thought "uppers" were the top part of my dentures.

✧ ✧ ✧ ✧ ✧

For convenience sake, an elderly married couple scheduled their annual physical examinations to take place on the same day.

After examining the elderly man, the doctor said, "You appear to be in good health. Are there any medical concerns you would like to discuss with me?"

"Yes, doctor, there is one," replied the elderly man. "After I make love to my wife for the first time, I am usually hot and sweaty. And then, after I have sex with my wife the second time, I am usually cold and chilly."

"That's quite interesting," replied the doctor. "Let me do some research and get back to you."

After examining the elderly lady, the doctor said, "Everything appears to be fine. Are there any medical concerns you would like to discuss with me?"

The lady assured the doctor that she didn't have any questions or concerns.

The doctor then asked, "Your husband had quite an unusual concern. He claims that he is usually hot and sweaty after making love the first time and then cold and chilly after the second time. Do you have any idea why this would be?"

108 / Laugh Your Lips Off!

"Oh, that silly old fool," she replied. "That's because the first time is usually in July and the second time is usually in December!"

✧ ✧ ✧ ✧ ✧

A couple were celebrating their 60th wedding anniversary. They had wed as childhood sweethearts and moved back to their old neighborhood after they retired.

Holding hands, they walked back to their old school. It was not locked, so they entered, and wandered the classrooms until they found the old desk they'd shared where Andy had carved "I love you, Sally."

On their way back home an armored car passed by and a bag of money fell out. They picked it up and not knowing what to do with it, they took it home. There, they counted the money: $100,000.

Andy said, "We've got to give it back!"

Sally said, "Finders keepers," and put the money back into the bag and hid it in their attic.

The next day, two FBI men were canvassing the neighborhood looking for the money and knocked on the door. "Pardon me, did either of you find a bag that fell out of an armored car yesterday?"

Sally said, "No."

Andy said, "She's lying. She hid it in the attic!"

Sally said, "Don't believe him, he's getting senile."

The agents turned to Andy and began to question him. One said, "Tell us the story from the beginning."

Andy said, "Well, when Sally and I were walking home from school yesterday...."

The first FBI agent interrupted him with a heavy sigh and turned to his partner. "I told you this was a waste of time. Let's go."

✧ ✧ ✧ ✧ ✧

I have always dreaded old age. I cannot imagine anything worse than being old.... How awful it must be to have nothing to do all day long but stare at the walls or watch TV.

So last week, when the mayor suggested we all celebrate Senior Citizen Week by cheering up a senior citizen, I determined to do just that. I would call on my new neighbor, an elderly retired gentleman, recently widowed, who, I presumed, had moved in with his married daughter because he was too old to take care of himself.

I baked a batch of brownies, and, without bothering to call (some old people cannot hear the phone), I went off to brighten this old guy's day.

When I rang the doorbell this "old guy" came to the door dressed in tennis shorts and a polo shirt, looking about as ancient and decrepit as Donny Osmond.

"I'm sorry I can't invite you in," he said when I introduced myself, "but I'm due at the Racquet Club at two.

110 / Laugh Your Lips Off!

I'm playing in the semi-finals today."

"Oh, that's OK," I said. "I baked you some brownies."

"Great!" he interrupted, snatching the box. "Just what I need for bridge club tomorrow! Thanks so much!"

"...and just thought we'd visit a while. But that's OK! I'll just run across the street and call on Granny Grady...."

"Don't bother," he said. "Gran's not home; I know. I just called to remind her of our date to go dancing tonight. She may be at the beauty shop. She mentioned at breakfast that she had an appointment for a tint job."

I called my mother's cousin (age 83); she was in the hospital ... working in the gift shop. I called my aunt (age 74); she was on vacation in China. I called my husband's uncle (age 79). He was on his honeymoon.

I still dread old age, now more than ever. I just don't think I'm up to it.

✧ ✧ ✧ ✧ ✧

A guy shopping in a supermarket noticed a little old lady following him around. If he stopped, she stopped. Furthermore she kept staring at him.

She finally overtook him at the checkout, and she turned to him and said, "I hope I haven't made you feel ill at ease; it's just that you look so much like my late son."

He answered, "That's OK."

"I know it's silly, but if you'd call out 'Goodbye, Mom' as I leave the store, it would make me feel so happy."

She then went through the checkout just ahead of him, and as she was on her way out of the store, the man called out, "Goodbye, Mom." The little old lady waved and smiled back at him.

Pleased that he had brought a little sunshine into someone's day, he went to pay for his groceries. "That comes to $121.85," said the clerk.

"How come so much?" the man asked. "I only bought milk, bread and lunch meat."

The clerk replied, "Yeah, but your mother said you'd pay for her things, too."

✧ ✧ ✧ ✧ ✧

An elderly woman and her little grandson, whose face was sprinkled with bright freckles, spent the day at the zoo. Lots of children were waiting in line to get their cheeks painted by a local artist who was decorating them with tiger paws.

"You've got so many freckles, there's no place to paint!" a girl in the line said to the little fella.

Embarrassed, the little boy dropped his head. His grandmother knelt down next to him. "I love your freckles. When I was a little girl I always wanted freckles, she said, while tracing her finger across the child's cheek. "Freckles are beautiful!"

The boy looked up, "Really?"

"Of course," said the grandmother. "Why, just name me one thing that's prettier than freckles."

The little boy thought for a moment, peered intensely into his grandma's face and softly whispered, "Wrinkles."

✧ ✧ ✧ ✧ ✧

If My Body Were a Car

If my body were a car, I would be thinking about trading it in for a newer model. I've got bumps and dents and scratches in my finish and my paint job is getting a little dull, but that's not the worst of it:

- My headlights are out of focus and it's especially hard to see things up close.

- My traction is not as graceful as it once was. I slip and slide and skid and bump into things even in the best of weather.

- My whitewalls are stained with varicose veins.

- It takes me hours to reach my maximum speed.

- My fuel rate burns inefficiently.

- But here's the worst of it – almost every time I sneeze, cough or sputter ... either my radiator leaks or my exhaust backfires!

"You may not be able to change a situation, but with humor you can change your attitude about it." — *Allen Klein*

17
A Little Holy Humor

Does God have a sense of humor? Of course He does! After all, He created platypuses, hyenas, bullfrogs and humans, didn't He? Here are some of my favorite jokes and stories with the Big Guy in mind....

✧ ✧ ✧ ✧ ✧

The preacher's 5-year-old daughter noticed that he always paused and bowed his head for a moment before starting his sermon. One day she asked him why.

"Well, honey," he began, proud his daughter was so observant of his messages, "I'm asking the Lord to help me preach a good sermon."

114 / Laugh Your Lips Off!

"Well," his daughter said, "How come he doesn't do it?"

✧ ✧ ✧ ✧ ✧

A woman was mailing an old family Bible to her brother in another part of the country when the postal clerk asked her, "Is there anything breakable in here?"

"Just the Ten Commandments," she replied.

✧ ✧ ✧ ✧ ✧

A man in Topeka, Kansas decided to write a book about churches around the country. He started by flying to San Francisco and started working east from there.

Going to a very large church, he began taking photographs and making notes.

He spotted a golden telephone on the vestibule wall and was intrigued with a sign, which read "Calls: $10,000 a minute."

Seeking out the pastor he asked about the phone and the sign. The pastor answered that this golden phone is, in fact, a direct line to Heaven and if he pays the price he can talk directly to GOD.

The man thanked the pastor and continued on his way. As he continued to visit churches in Seattle, Dallas, Chicago, Milwaukee, and many cities and towns all around the United States, he found more phones, with the same sign, and the same answer from each pastor.

Finally, he arrived in Tennessee, upon entering a church

in the beautiful mountainous region of Tennessee, behold — he saw the usual golden telephone. But THIS time, the sign read, "Calls: 35 cents."

Fascinated, he asked to talk to the pastor, "Reverend, I have been in cities all across the country and in each church I have found this golden telephone and have been told it is a direct line to Heaven and that I could talk to GOD, but in the other churches the cost was $10,000 a minute. Your sign reads only 35 cents a call. Why?"

The pastor, smiling broadly, replied, "Son, you're in Tennessee now ... You're in God's Country. It's a local call."

(Editor's note ... I've collected several versions of this joke, with the "Holy Ground State" varying depending on the source. Seems we all have a little home-state pride!)

✧ ✧ ✧ ✧ ✧

A Sunday School class was learning about the Good Samaritan.

To make the story vivid to the children, the teacher told the story in detail, describing how the Samaritan was beaten, robbed, then left for dead.

Then she asked the class what they would do if they saw someone on the side of the road, beaten and all bloody.

A little girl quietly replied, "I think I'd throw up."

✧ ✧ ✧ ✧ ✧

116 / Laugh Your Lips Off!

A Sunday school teacher asked, "Joey, do you think Noah did a lot of fishing when he was on the Ark?"

"No," said Joey. "How could he, with just two worms?"

✧ ✧ ✧ ✧ ✧

I was testing my Sunday school class to see if they understood the concept of getting to Heaven. I asked them, "If I sold my house and my car, had a big garage sale and gave all my money to the church, would that get me into Heaven?"

"NO!" the children answered.

"If I cleaned the church every day, mowed the yard, and kept everything neat and tidy, would that get me into Heaven?"

Again, the answer was, "NO!"

By now I was starting to smile. Hey, this was fun!

"Well, then, if I was kind to animals and gave candy to all the children, and loved my husband, would that get me into Heaven?"

I asked them again. Again, they all answered, "NO!"

I was just bursting with pride for them. "Well," I continued, "then how can I get into Heaven?"

A 6-year-old boy shouted out,

"YOU GOTTA BE DEAD."

✧ ✧ ✧ ✧ ✧

God Vs. the Scientist

The scientist approached God and said, "Listen, we've decided we no longer need you. Nowadays, we can extract stem cells, clone people, transplant hearts, and all kinds of things that were once considered miraculous."

God patiently heard him out, and then said, "All right. To see whether or not you still need me, why don't we have a little man-making contest!"

"OK, great!" the scientist said.

"Now, we're going to do this just like I did back in the old days with Adam," God said.

"That's fine," replied the scientist and he bent down to scoop up a handful of dirt.

"Whoa there!" God said, shaking His head. "Not so fast, pal.... You get your own dirt."

118 / Laugh Your Lips Off!

A Rabbi said to a precocious 6-year-old boy, "So your mother says your prayers for you each night? What does she say?"

"Thank God he's in bed!" the little boy answered.

✧ ✧ ✧ ✧ ✧

One Sunday morning, a mother went in to wake her son and tell him it was time to get ready for church, to which he replied, "I'm not going."

"Why not?" she asked."

"I'll give you two good reasons," he said. "One, they don't like me, and two, I don't like them."

His mother replied, "I'll give YOU two good reasons why you SHOULD go to church. One, you're 54 years old, and two, you're the pastor!"

✧ ✧ ✧ ✧ ✧

A 6-year-old boy was overheard reciting the Lord's prayer: "And forgive us our trash passes as we forgive those who passed trash against us."

✧ ✧ ✧ ✧ ✧

A Jewish Rabbi and a Catholic Priest met at the town's annual 4th of July picnic. Old friends, they began their usual banter.

"This baked ham is really delicious," the priest teased the rabbi.

"You really ought to try it. I know it's against your religion, but I can't understand why such a wonderful food should be forbidden! You don't know what you're missing. You just haven't lived until you've tried Mrs. Hall's prized Virginia Baked Ham. Tell me, Rabbi, when are you going to break down and try it?"

The rabbi looked at the priest with a big grin, and said, "At your wedding."

✧ ✧ ✧ ✧ ✧

An elderly woman walked into the local country church. The friendly usher greeted her at the door and helped her up the flight of steps. "Where would you like to sit?" he asked politely.

"As close to the front as possible," the woman said.

"You really don't want to do that," the usher said in a confidential tone. "The preacher is really boring."

"Do you happen to know who I am?" the woman inquired rather loudly.

"No," the usher said.

"I'm the pastor's mother," she replied indignantly.

"Oh ... do you know who I am?" the usher asked.

"No," the pastor's mother said.

"Good," the usher answered.

✧ ✧ ✧ ✧ ✧

120 / Laugh Your Lips Off!

A priest, a minister and a guru sat discussing the best positions for prayer, while a telephone repairman worked nearby.

"Kneeling is definitely the best way to pray," the priest said.

"No," said the minister. "I get the best results standing with my hands outstretched to Heaven."

"You're both wrong," the guru said. "The most effective prayer position is lying face down on the floor."

The repairman could contain himself no longer. "Hey, fellas," he interrupted. "The best prayin' I ever did was while hangin' upside down from a telephone pole."

✧ ✧ ✧ ✧ ✧

"Anyone with needs to be prayed over, come forward, to the front of the altar," the preacher declared.

Leroy got in line, and when it was his turn, the preacher asked: "Son, what do you want me to pray about for you?"

"Preacher, I need you to pray for my hearing," said the man.

The preacher put his hands over Leroy's ears and prays. After a few minutes, the preacher removes his hands, stands back and asks, "Leroy, how is your hearing now?"

"Well, I don't know, Reverend," said Leroy. "My hearing isn't until next Wednesday."

✧ ✧ ✧ ✧ ✧

A mother asked her young daughter what she had learned in Sunday School.

The girl answered, "Don't be scared, you'll get your quilt."

The mom was a bit perplexed. So when she ran into the Sunday School teacher in the grocery store the next day, she asked her what the lesson had been.

The teacher replied, "Do not be afraid; thy comforter is coming."

✧ ✧ ✧ ✧ ✧

122 / Laugh Your Lips Off!

"Everything is funny, as long as it's happening to somebody else."
— *Will Rogers*

18
Assorted Grins, Giggles & Guffaws

If carrots are so good for your eyes, how come I see so many dead rabbits along the highway?

✧ ✧ ✧ ✧ ✧

The captain called the Sergeant in. "Sarge, I just got a telegram that Private Jones' mother died yesterday. Better go tell him and send him in to see me." So the Sergeant calls for his morning formation and lines up all the troops.

124 / Laugh Your Lips Off!

"Listen up, men," says the Sergeant. "Johnson, report to the mess hall for KP. Smith, report to Personnel to sign some papers. The rest of you men report to the Motor Pool for maintenance. Oh, by the way, Jones, your mother died, report to the commander."

Later that day the Captain called the Sergeant into his office. "Hey, Sarge, that was a pretty cold way to inform Jones his mother died. Couldn't you be a bit more tactful next time?"

"Yes, sir," answered the Sarge.

A few months later, the Captain called the Sergeant in again with, "Sarge, I just got a telegram that Private McGrath's mother died. You'd better go tell him and send him in to see me. This time be more tactful."

So the Sergeant calls for his morning formation. "OK, men, fall in and listen up. Everybody with a mother, take two steps forward.... Not so fast, McGrath!"

✧ ✧ ✧ ✧ ✧

The new supermarket near our house has an automatic mist machine to keep the produce fresh. Just before it goes on, you hear the sound of a thunderstorm.

When you approach the milk cases, you hear cows mooing. When you approach the egg case, you hear hens cackle.

So far I've been too afraid to go down the toilet paper aisle.

✧ ✧ ✧ ✧ ✧

Not many people know that the great American inventor Thomas Edison was an avid fisherman.

He usually included some trout fishing on his infrequent vacations. During one such trip to the West, he was befriended by an native american tribe. They provided free room and board, plus expert fishing guides for his stay.

On his first night, he learned that the only "restroom" was an old-fashioned outhouse which had no light, even though the village had electricity in the homes.

To thank the tribe for their kindness during his stay, Edison purchased the necessary materials and personally installed lighting in the privy.

Thus, he became the first person to wire a head for a reservation.

✧ ✧ ✧ ✧ ✧

Two sisters, one blonde and one brunette, inherit the family ranch. Unfortunately, they soon find they are in financial trouble. To keep the bank from repossessing the ranch they need to purchase a bull from a stockyard in a far-away town so that they can breed their own stock. They only have $600 left.

Upon leaving, the brunette tells her sister, "When I get there, if I decide to buy the bull, I'll contact you to drive out after me and haul it home."

126 / Laugh Your Lips Off!

The brunette arrives at the stockyard, inspects the bull, and decides she wants it. The man tells her he will sell it for $599. After paying him, she drives to the nearest town to send her sister a telegram to tell her the news.

She walks into the telegraph office, and says, "I want to send a telegram to my sister saying I've bought a bull for our ranch. I need her to hitch the trailer to our pick-up truck and drive out here so we can haul it home."

The telegraph operator explains that he'll be glad to help her, then adds, "It's just 99 cents a word." Well, after paying for the bull, the brunette only has $1 left. She realizes that she'll only be able to send her sister one word. After a few minutes, she nods and says, "I want you to send her the word "comfortable."

The operator shakes his head. "How will she know that you want her to hitch the trailer to your pickup truck and drive out here to haul that bull back to your ranch if you send her just the word 'comfortable?'"

The brunette explains, "My sister's blonde. The word's big. She'll read it very slowly... 'com-for-da-bull.'"

✧ ✧ ✧ ✧ ✧

A young man goes out and buys the best car available: a 2012 Turbo BeepBeep. Price tag: $500,000.

An old man on a moped pulls up next to him and says, "What kind of car ya' got there, sonny?"

The young many replies "A 2012 Turbo BeepBeep. They cost $500,000."

"Why is it so expensive?" asks the old man.

"Because this car can do up to 320 miles an hour!" states the cool dude proudly.

So, the old man pokes his head in the window and looks around. Leaning back, he says, "That's a pretty nice car, all right!" Just then the light changes, so the guy with the new car floors it.

Suddenly, he notices a dot in his rear view mirror. It's getting closer! Something whips by him, even though his speedometer reads 320 mph. "What on earth could be going faster than my Turbo BeepBeep?" he asks.

Then, ahead of him, he sees a dot coming back toward him. Whooosshh! It goes by again! And, it almost looked like the old man on the moped!

"Couldn't be," thinks the guy. "How could a moped outrun a Turbo BeepBeep?"

Again, he sees a dot in his rearview mirror! Whatever it is plows straight into the back of his new car.

The young man jumps out, and sees it is the old man on the moped! The young man says, "You're hurt bad! Is there anything I can do for you?"

The old man groans and replies "Yes, sonny. If you don't mind, could ya unhook my suspenders from your side-view mirror?"

✧ ✧ ✧ ✧ ✧

128 / Laugh Your Lips Off!

Did you hear about the smalltown police station that got hit by a burglary? Someone stole all the toilets. The police say they have absolutely nothing to go on.

✧ ✧ ✧ ✧ ✧

As the newest member of the church ladies' group, Alice jumped at the chance to help at the bake sale. Unfortunately, she forgot about the event until the morning of the bake sale. Quickly rummaging through cabinets, she found an old angel food cake mix and made it while drying her hair, ironing her work outfit and helping her son pack his lunch.

But when Alice took the cake from the oven the center had dropped flat and the cake was horribly disfigured.

So, being inventive and not wanting anyone to think she was not the perfect woman able to handle all things at all times or that, God forbid, she not participate in the bake sale, she looked for something to build up the center of the cake. She grabbed the only thing she could find — a roll of toilet paper — plunked it in and covered it with icing. The cake looked beautiful!

Before taking the cake to church and heading to work, Alice woke her teen-age daughter and gave her $20 and specific instructions to be at the bake sale the minute it opened at 9:30 a.m., buy that cake and bring it home.

When the daughter arrived at the sale, she found that it had in fact begun at 9 a.m., and that her mom's perfect cake had already been sold. She grabbed her cell phone and called her mom.

Alice was beside herself. Everyone would know ... what should she do? All night Alice lay awake thinking about people pointing their fingers at her and talking.

The next day, Alice promised herself that she would try not to think about the cake and would attend a fancy bridal shower and try to have a good time.

Alice did not really want to attend because the hostess was a snob who spent much too much time telling others all about her perfect husband, children, home and life. But she tried to focus on the fact that the party would be about the bride-to-be, not the hostess.

The party in the snobby woman's home was beyond elegant, with candles and fresh flowers everywhere. And there, amid all the beautiful wedding-themed decorations, perched on a stunning crystal cake stand, was ... *Alice's bake sale cake!*

Alice felt the blood drain from her face when she saw the cake. She started to get out of her chair to rush into the kitchen to tell her hostess all about it, but before she could get to her feet, one of the guests commented, "What a beautiful cake!"

Alice who was still stunned and trying to formulate what words she would use to explain the situation, sat back in her chair when she heard the hostess reply in her haughtiest tone, "Thank you, I baked it myself."

As the guests ooh'ed and aah'ed over the cake, Alice simply smiled and said, in all honesty, "God is good."

✧ ✧ ✧ ✧ ✧

A Few of Life's Little Mysteries

- Does a clean house indicate that there is a broken computer in it?

- Why is it that no matter the color of bubble bath, the bubbles are always white?

- Is there ever a day when mattresses are NOT on sale?

- Why do people constantly return to the refrigerator with the hopes that something new to eat will have materialized?

- On electric toasters, why do they engrave the message "one slice"? How many pieces of bread do they think people are really gonna try to stuff in that slot?

- Why do people keep running over a string with their vacuum cleaner, then reach down, pick it up, examine it, and put it down to give their vacuum one more chance?

- Why is it that no plastic garbage bag will open from the end you first try?

- How do those dead bugs get into closed light fixtures?

- Why do we wash BATH towels? Aren't we clean when we use them? If not then what was the purpose of the bath?

- Considering all the lint you get in your dryer, if you kept drying your clothes would they eventually just disappear?

- When we are in the supermarket and someone rams our ankle with a shopping cart then apologizes for doing so, why do we say 'It's all right"? It isn't all right, so why don't we say, "That hurt, you stupid idiot?"

- Why is it that when you're walking up the stairs and you get to the top you always think there's still one more step?

- Why is it that whenever you attempt to catch something that's falling off the table you always manage to knock something else over?

- Is it true that the only difference between a yard sale and a trash pickup is how close to the road the stuff is placed?

- In winter, why do we try to keep the house as warm as it was in summer when we complained about the heat?

- Why do old men wear their pants higher than younger men?

- Why is it that men can react to broken bones as "just a sprain" and deep wounds as "just a scratch", but when they get the sniffles they are deathly ill "with the flu" and have to be bedridden for weeks?

- How come we never hear any father-in-law jokes?

- Why is it that inside every older person is a younger person wondering what the heck happened?

132 / Laugh Your Lips Off!

> "Humor is a presence in the world, like grace, and shines on everyone."
> — Garrison Keillor

19
A Few for Ole & Lena Fans

Two young Norwegians from up in Minnesota were looking at a Sears catalog and admiring the models.

Ole said to Sven, "Have ya seen da beautiful girls in this catalog?"

Sven replied, "Yah, they are very beautiful. And look at the prices!"

Ole says, with wide eyes, "Wow, dat's not dat bad. At this price, I'm buying one."

Sven smiled and patted him on the back. "Good idea!

134 / Laugh Your Lips Off!

Order one and if she's as beautiful as she is in the catalog, I'll get one for me."

A week later, Sven asked his friend Ole, "Did ya ever receive dat girl you ordered from da Sears catalog?"

Ole replied, "Not yet, but it shouldn't be long now. I got her clothes in da mail yesterday!"

✧ ✧ ✧ ✧ ✧

Ole and Lena were dating when they decided to go to the Olympics. Seeing the fit young Ole in the bleachers during the track-and-field events, a tourist asked him, "Are you a pole vaulter?"

Ole said, "No, I'm Norvegian and my name ain't Valter."

✧ ✧ ✧ ✧ ✧

Ole and Lena got married. On their honeymoon trip they were nearing Minneapolis when Ole put his hand on Lena's knee. Giggling, Lena said, "We're married now, Ole. You can go a little farther now if ya vant to."

So Ole drove to Duluth.

✧ ✧ ✧ ✧ ✧

For their first wedding anniversary, Ole bought Lena a piano. A few weeks later, his fishing buddy, Lars, asked how Lena was doing with the piano.

"Oh," said Ole. "I persuaded her to svitch to a clarinet."

"How come?" asked Lars.

"Vell," said Ole. "Because vith a clarinet she can't sing."

✧ ✧ ✧ ✧ ✧

Ole and Lena were on their first train ride. They were served exotic food on this trip as well, and Ole was peeling his first banana as the train neared a tunnel.

Suddenly Ole shouted, "Lena! Did you eat your banana yet?"

"No, Ole, why?"

"Vell, don't touch it, den," Ole exclaimed. "I yust took vun bite and vent blind!"

✧ ✧ ✧ ✧ ✧

Government surveyors came to Ole's farm in the fall and asked if they could do some surveying. Ole agreed and Lena even served them a nice meal at noontime.

The next spring, the two surveyors stopped by and told Ole, "Because you were so kind to us, we wanted to give you this bad news in person instead of by letter."

Ole replied, "Vhat's da bad news?"

136 / Laugh Your Lips Off!

The surveyors stated, "Well, after our work we discovered your farm is not in Minnesota, but is actually in South Dakota!"

To the surveyors' surprise, Ole laughed and clapped his hands. "Why, dat's da best news I heard in a long time," said Ole. "Why I was yust tellin' Lena this morning, 'I don't tink I can take anudder winter in Minnesota."

✧ ✧ ✧ ✧ ✧

Lars: "Ole, stand in front of my car and tell me if da turn signals are verking."

Ole: "Yes, no, yes, no, yes, no, yes, no...."

✧ ✧ ✧ ✧ ✧

One summer when it was too hot to work in the fields, Ole decided to surprise Lena by finally painting the kitchen like she'd been wanting him to do.

Lena got home from town to find a beautiful new kitchen — and Ole, passed out on the floor, covered in perspiration and wearing both his heavy winter parka and her knee-length wool coat.

"Ole, are you OK? Vhat are you doing?" she asked as she shook him awake.

"Oh ..." said Ole, as he came around. "I vanted to do a good job, so I vas sure to follow da directions exactly."

Still confused, Lena picked up the paint can and read: "For best results, put on two coats."

✧ ✧ ✧ ✧ ✧

After a long, happy life, Ole died. So Lena went to the local paper to put a notice in the obituaries. The obituary writer, after offering his condolences, asked Lena what she would like to say about her husband of more than 50 years.

Lena replied, "You yust put, 'Ole died.'"

The writer, somewhat perplexed, asked, "That's it? Just 'Ole died?' Surely there must be something more you'd like to say about Ole. If it's money you're concerned about, the first five words are free. We must say something more."

So Lena pondered for a few minutes and finally said, "OK, you put, 'Ole died. Boat for sale.'"

✧ ✧ ✧ ✧ ✧

138 / Laugh Your Lips Off!

> "Wrinkles should merely indicate where smiles have been."
> — Mark Twain

20
Sending You Off With a Smile

Thank you for joining me on this little joy-inducing journey! I hope you've enjoyed the trip (without drugs!).

I can't think of a sweeter way to end this book than to include my very own masterpieces!

A few years ago, I was invited to submit a short story to possibly be included in "Chicken Soup for the Nurse's Soul #2." I decided to play it safe and submitted THREE stories! (FYI, none of them made it into the book!) but I am sharing them here.

140 / Laugh Your Lips Off!

I hope they each underscore in a different way the power that humor has as a coping mechanism and as a tool to bridge the gap when words fail.

The first story, **"How Do You 'Smell' Relief?"** is one that still brings tears of laughter to my eyes as I remember one of my many embarrassing moments as a teen-age nursing student.

The second, **"Heaven ... or Hell?"** recalls my life-changing experience as a clown ambassador on a mission trip to China with the famous Dr. Patch Adams.

And finally, I close with a story, **"A Good Trade,"** that brings up one of my fondest memories of my nursing career.

Enjoy! ~ Jenny

✧ ✧ ✧ ✧ ✧

How Do You 'Smell' Relief?

When I think of my nurse's training, I'm reminded of the long hours, the hard work, and of being scared to death most of the time — all aspects that I expect haven't changed much in the five decades since.

Still, as difficult as nursing school was, the other students and I seemed to find fun. Sometimes, just sharing stories of our fledgling nursing experiences left us in stitches! I had an experience in my junior year that not only made for snickers around the dormitory that night, but that still brings laughs when I share it today.

I had been assigned a patient who needed a soapsuds enema. By now, this procedure was "old hat" to me. I could do it with my eyes closed ... or so I thought.

I administered the enema exactly as I had been taught — carefully positioning my patient on her left side, letting the solution run in slowly, all the while instructing my patient to take deep breaths (to lessen any possibility of cramping), then helping her onto the bedpan and making sure she was comfortable before I left for class. I told her I would be back as soon as I could ... but I neglected to tell her my class was an hour long.

An hour later, I hurried back to check the results.

Fortunately for my patient (and probably for me, as well), some person had removed the bedpan from underneath her.

Unfortunately for my patient and for everyone else on the ward, that person hadn't emptied the bedpan. Instead — probably realizing that I would want to see the results — the person had balanced the bedpan on top of the cast-iron heat register.

For 60 minutes or so, the results of my carefully administered soapsuds enema had been ... "simmering."

All nurses are taught to chart enema results as either "good," "fair" or "poor." Too bad for me, that didn't include "well done."

✧ ✧ ✧ ✧ ✧

Heaven ... or Hell?

My career as a healthcare provider — nurse, educator, and manager of a home emergency system — spans five decades filled with countless stories and faces. What really stands out in my mind is my 12-day trip to China in September 2000 that changed my life as a member of a Fun Medicine Delegation led by the world-famous clown/physician Dr. Patch Adams.

My 44 companions and I left American soil dressed in our clown personas and stayed that way almost exclusively until we returned.

In a place where many people had never seen a clown before, we traveled in our colorful costumes, painted faces, oversized shoes and hot, bright wigs throughout the 12 days of 90-degree weather and 90-percent humidity. We shared giggles with thousands of persons from our host country — hoisting tiny children upon our laps at orphanages, drawing and entertaining crowds in every public square and starting a conga line with residents at a home for the elderly.

So many faces! So much walking and dancing and smiling! So many opportunities to share our joy of life and our message that humor can be a great healer — all in a country where they seemed to have the "work ethic" down pat, but couldn't quite grasp the "play ethic."

Then came our visit to a hospice in Beijing.

What a stark contrast — 45 brightly colored clowns traipsing into this dark, primitive, cheerless building where people lay on thin mattresses in tiny cubicles, alone, waiting to die.

After gathering in a group while Dr. Patch Adams explained our mission to the staff, we spread out to interact with our assigned patients, one on one.

I went into my assigned area as quietly as my bright red shoes would allow. I entered my patient's cubicle and approached the small, still figure on the cot. The elderly man lay unmoving, covered in a wool blanket and wearing wool socks in the oppressive heat, hands folded across his chest.

At first, I did what every good nurse does — an assessment. Squinting through the dark, windowless room, I measured his respirations and assessed his skin color. His breathing, while shallow, was consistent. His eyes were closed.

Then, I switched into clown mode, reminding myself: "Jenny, you've come halfway across the world to spread some cheer ... so get to it!" Still, my inner pep talk did little to boost my confidence in this situation, when my task seemed insurmountable.

I took a deep breath, walked up to him, leaned down, and, doing my best not to startle him, gently put my hand upon his folded hands on his chest.

Immediately — almost as if I had flipped an electric switch on his eyelids — his eyes FLEW open! The dark pupils locked onto mine. His surprised, searching eyes took me in — clown makeup, bright yellow wig, red nose and all — but his expression never changed.

144 / Laugh Your Lips Off!

He lay there, completely deadpan, except for eyes that seemed to be searching for something familiar in this totally foreign moment.

Can you imagine what was going through his mind? "Where am I? Have I died and gone to heaven ... or hell? Who ... or what ... is this thing in my face?"

I had no clue how to proceed. Again, I turned to my nurse's training. Slowly, gently, I began stroking his weathered hands with my own, sharing some "touch therapy." I kept doing so for several minutes in the dark room. I smiled. Soon, I noticed that I had begun to hum. For some reason, the tune, "I Love a Parade," was lilting through my lips.

Still no expression change on my patient's part. His face was emotionless, but his eyes had that "Where am I? What is happening? Where am I?" look to them.

All of a sudden I noticed water on my hands. I furrowed my brow, wondering where the water could be coming from. Then I realized it was coming from me! Sweat was dripping off my face like a faucet. I knew that if I didn't get out of there — very soon — I would pass out and end up on top of that poor man.

So I began to step backward toward the door, waving a tiny wave and smiling, until I was out of his sight.

To this day, I have no idea what kind of an impact I made on this patient. We exchanged not a word. All I did was administer a little touch therapy, music therapy, plus a lot of hydrotherapy. In my heart, I have to believe that I reached him, even though he didn't seem to acknowledge it. I was satisfied. I'd done the best I could.

If nothing else, at least I had provided a little dying man with a big distraction — and quite the story to tell his next visitor!

✧ ✧ ✧ ✧ ✧

A Good Trade

As a 19-year-old female student nurse born and raised in a small South Dakota town, I found myself facing new — and often intimidating — experiences every day. It was 1953, and I was working in a small general hospital in Sioux City, Iowa, learning my trade.

This particular day, I faced a number of "firsts" all wrapped up in the same patient. First time in the eight-bed men's ward, first time caring for a male patient close to my own age, first time caring for a person of a different race than myself. (This is no biggie nowadays, but please keep in mind that the time was the 1950s, the setting was Iowa and the student nurse involved — me — was intimidated to even be in the men's ward, not to mention feeling quite inadequate when it came to providing real, live patients with actual clinical care).

This was in the day when hospitals had separate men's and women's wards with several beds in a single large room. The only way to provide any sort of patient privacy was to wheel a screen between the beds.

I had to garner up a lot of courage to give this man the care he needed while also appearing competent and professional — when I was feeling anything but!

146 / Laugh Your Lips Off!

This young man was on complete bed rest requiring total care. And here he was, poor fellow, assigned ME to provide that care! Thankfully, my nurse's training kicked in, and, rather hesitantly, I introduced myself. "Good morning, my name is Jenny, and I'm here to give you your bed bath."

My patient's face showed some of the same emotions I was feeling — "Oh, this IS going to be awkward!"

We were both uncomfortable. Luckily, I'm a nervous talker. When I get nervous, boy, can I talk! So I started asking questions….

"Where you from?" … "Any brothers and sisters?" … "Are you still in school?" … and on I rambled.

His answers came stutteringly at first, but soon, we were chatting comfortably, even laughing (although much of it was nervous laughter), but the laughter broke the ice and boy, did it help break down barriers. The awkwardness was starting to disappear and a bonding was taking place.

When I had finished my tasks — feeling much more competent and at ease, I might add — I asked that all-important question: "Is there anything else I can do for you before I leave?" He looked around the stark surroundings — plain walls, white beds, white curtains on wheels, steel gray equipment — then looked me and said: "Is there any way you could get me a magazine or something to help pass the time away?"

His question put me into his shoes for just a moment — the shoes of a young man, frightened for his health, far from loved ones, alone in a strange environment with few people to visit with and nothing much to do.

I, too, was far from loved ones, but had many new friends to help me spend what little free time I had. To keep me company when I studied, I had a smart little alarm clock/radio — a gift from my parents when I left for nursing school, and a much-treasured possession.

I got an idea.

"You think you might like to listen to the radio?" I asked. He said he sure would, but didn't own one. And with no family or friends in town, he couldn't think of anyone to call to bring a radio, a book or anything else.

So I told my new friend I'd be back with a surprise. I noted a little spark of anxiety in his eyes when I said the word "surprise!"

I went to my dorm room and tucked the cherished radio under my coat. I headed back to the hospital, scampered up the steps and into the men's ward. With two hands, I held out the radio to my patient and said, "Here! Why don't you borrow my radio while you're here?"

The smile on his face — probably half joy from seeing the radio and half relief in realizing the "surprise" I had promised had nothing to do with a needle or bed pan — was heartwarming. I can still see him grinning from ear to ear, his eyes sparkling with joy.

I cleared a spot on his bedside table for the little radio, then plugged it in and showed him how to tune in local stations. Then I said goodbye and told him I'd stop in and see him as often as I could, and pick up the radio

148 / Laugh Your Lips Off!

when he was dismissed.

Several days went by and I got busy with my class schedule and work assignments. Finally, when I found time to get back to the men's ward, I walked up to the bed my friend had occupied, peeked around the curtain — and saw a stripped, empty bed. The bedside table was cleared off, too — except for my radio.

My radio — in three pieces.

My heart sunk — my prized possession, gone! I slowly, unbelievingly, walked up to the bedside table. Disappointment flooded over me. The lump in my throat grew bigger with each step. I thought I might even cry...

Then I saw a half-sheet of paper tucked under the radio. Written in sharp, staccato pencil was a brief note:

> Dear Nurse Jenny,
>
> Sorry about your radio. It fell on the floor and broke. Thanks for letting me use it.
>
> You are a good nurse. ~ Jim

I was sad to see my radio in pieces. But the tears that came after reading the note weren't because of what I had lost. They were for what I had learned: In nursing, it sometimes takes a bit of sacrifice to bring a smile to a patient's face.

And that smile is worth more than just about anything.

Jenny Herrick, August 15, 2012

Jenny Herrick believes you should laugh heartily and often — not just for the heck of it, but for the health of it!

Living proof that a sense of humor can buoy you through life's toughest challenges, Jenny enjoys sharing her message as a nationally recognized humorist, motivational speaker and author.

Check out her side-splitting autobiography, **You Laugh, I'll Drive!** available at www.allkiddingaside.biz.

A native of Watertown, S.D., and lifelong Midwesterner, Jenny has done just about everything, from jerking sodas in South Dakota to injecting patients in Iowa to clowning at Ground Zero in New York. She traveled to Ground Zero as a clown to provide "mirth aid" to rescue workers, joined a Fun Medicine Delegation to China with Dr. Patch Adams and established a Caring Clown Troupe at her local hospital, where she continues to teach clown classes. She trained dogs to win top awards in the show ring and to bring comfort as pet therapy canines. A registered nurse, she is a Certified Laughter Leader, member of National Speakers Association, Toastmasters International, Clowns of America International, and the Applied Association for Therapeutic Humor.

To invite Jenny to speak at your next event or let her know what you think of her books, e-mail jenny @allkiddingaside.biz or write her at: All Kidding Aside, 2829 S. Cypress, Sioux City, IA, 51106. Check out her website at: www.allkiddingaside.biz

150 / Laugh Your Lips Off!

This is the second publishing venture in which Jenny Herrick has teamed up with her friend and colleague, **Kathy Hoeschen Massey,** a freelance writer, photographer and copy editor.

Originally from Alexandria, Minn., Kathy has called Sioux City, Iowa home since 1984. She enjoys putting her God-given talents to work helping others shine and share their gifts with others to make the burdens of this world a little lighter for us all.

When not collaborating with Jenny on her latest project, Kathy works as business administrator ("church mom") at Redeemer Lutheran Church in Sioux City. She and her husband, Ted, have two daughters, Katelyn and Courtney; two dogs, Buddy and Jazzy; one almost-son-in-law, Miguel, and one grandpuppy, Loka.

To reach Kathy and learn more about her business, Design On The Side, e-mail her at:
 kathyhmassey@gmail.com.

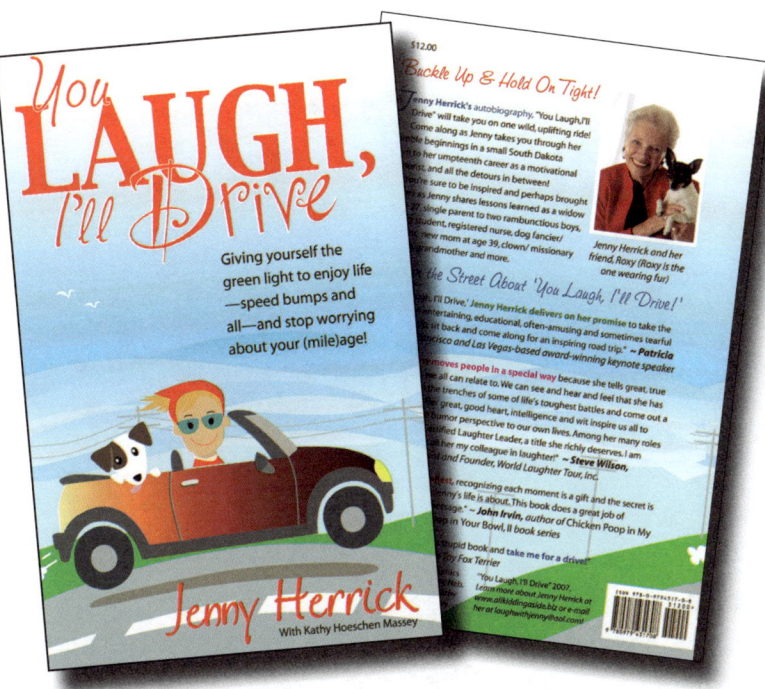

One last thought from Jenny...

Did you like my little joke book, **Laugh Your Lips Off!**? Then you'll love my autobiography, **You Laugh, I'll Drive!** It will take you on a wild, uplifting ride into how I've learned how to laugh, in spite of life's speed bumps, detours and head-on collisions.

To get your personally autographed copy of **You Laugh, I'll Drive,** or to have me speak to your group, please call me, e-mail me or visit my website today!

Keep on laughing!

Jenny Herrick
All Kidding Aside
2829 S. Cypress St.
Sioux City, IA 51106

Ph. 712.276.4315
E-mail: jenny@allkiddingaside.biz
Website: www.allkiddingaside.biz